DREAMS OF TRUTH AND BEAUTY

by

Fletcher N Brown

I0111184

Palm Tree Publishing

PALM TREE PUBLISHING
Wilmington, Delaware 19801

© Fletcher N Brown 2019

First published in United Kingdom
DECEMBER 2019

Typeset: Calibri 10pt-12pt

ISBN-10: 0 907282 77 6
ISBN-13: 9780907282778

The right of Fletcher Brown to be identified as the author of this work has been asserted in accordance with sections 77 and 78 of the Copyright Designs and Patents Act 1988 (UK)

DREAMS OF TRUTH AND BEAUTY

Poetic & Philosophical Works
by
Fletcher N Brown

Author's Note

———————

The texts which follow are, in part, an attempt to establish the foundations of a spiritual science, and a hymn of praise to Man's eternal nature. Whilst it has proven, for me, impossible to reconcile these purposes entirely, it is my firm belief that they converge upon a single point of fact: Beauty and Truth are the Alpha and Omega, respectively, of humanity's cosmic vocation. (Only Love, which is the hopeful seed and fruit of their conjunction, is greater in authority and awe.) It is my hope, therefore, that the reader might consider, equally, the poetry, stories and essays which comprise this volume, and seek out correspondences between them. Though one may feel greater affinity for this mode of function or that, understanding lies forever in the balance.

We may find balance, likewise, in the endeavor to transcend collective religious forms by utilizing what is called herein the

3

Natural Imagination: an innate individual power serving to reveal first-hand the mysteries of the spiritual dimension. This living, interior truth, with unique scriptures and nomenclature in each case, is the only spiritual Way wholly fit for a post-religious culture, such as ours has come to be in recent years. Whilst we have no religion, many of us retain a powerful spiritual impulse nonetheless, which compels us to seek out the primordial governing values and comprehend them in an objective sense. The essays herein serve to elucidate the process of arriving at the above conclusion, whilst the stories and poetry are each examples of its expression—prophecies and prayers, if you will—which comprise the scripture of my own Natural Imagination's production.

It is inevitable that such a volume contains its share of arcane terminology, though the determined reader may rest assured that all such terms, if invented herein, are explained in context or, if not, have a long heritage in the esoteric literature of one field of study or another. A simple web search will, in most cases, direct the reader down a veritable rabbit-hole of learning. It was the prerogative of Gurdjieff, the great mystic and teacher of dancing, to bury the dog (star) so deeply within his literary artifice that its exhumation should strengthen the will and reveal the seeker to herself. It has, at times, been my intention to follow in the great man's footsteps in this regard.

Should one decide that this collection, and the system it comprises, is too abstruse, and its author of too little repute, to warrant the detailed study required for its thorough understanding, I should like to pass along a single message; a single acorn in the dense summer branches, which they might take away for lasting nourishment: *meditate on what you truly yearn for, allowing nothing to constrain your imagination, such that you might realise the truth of your nature and destiny.* In so doing, one might chance to discover within themselves the True Desire, shared by all human beings past and present. Call it what you will—though I might chance to call it *harmony*—by this, and this alone, shall nations lay down arms and know each other to be brothers in spirit.

Dedication

This collection is dedicated to my mother, step-father and wife, who have lovingly afforded me the time and resources to write, revise and compile it. It is dedicated, likewise, without any diminution of the former, to those angels and devils who have lent their voices to my pen for the furtherance of God's work upon Earth.

Fletcher Brown

Contents

The Devils of Gehenna

In the early days of Gehenna, devils walked among men in the open fields, and showed themselves at night as reaching shadows. Those who walked along the grazelands saw them often, and some folk chanced to speak with them by moonlight. One man, called Garzibald, befriended their kind and offered a tithe of his flock in exchange for the devils' secret lore. This lore, called True Knowledge of the World-Soul, has been passed down through five hundred generations by means of direct psychical transmission, and has arrived upon my pen to show in part, so that those seekers of determined will might receive the knowledge of the devils of Gehenna as it was first conveyed to Garzibald by moonlight.

We knew no bounds in those days and lived freely by the mana of God, which we imbibed, and by its nutriment saw visions of the heavens and hells. These rose not high above, nor sank below, but existed in the midst of us, and the beings of those worlds beheld us likewise. They were neither born, nor did they die, but merely apparated and evaporated into a continuous aether which implicated and explicated its polymorphous potential in service of the Transcendent

Evolutionary Process, which suffuses all worlds to this day, and is called the Will of God by priests and magi.

The angels, who dwelt in the heavens, showed to us our nature in part, for they trusted us not with the True Knowledge of the World-Soul, believing we might perish should we hear it. Yet the devils, who were of hell, took no pity upon us and pleasured in the slaughter of illusions. Thus they told us we had never been born, and would not die when the life left our bodies. They revealed to us the nature of the World-Soul, and called us 'energy-manifest-in-time,' being specific instances of relevation[1] of the Transcendent Evolutionary Process as it operates within this, the plane of Mundus.

They told us, likewise, to unlearn the allegories of the angels, which pandered to the weakness of our minds and live instead in accordance with the Truth: that we are worlds within worlds, gods within God, born of spiritual energy and to energy would return. Our duty would be done, irrespective of whether we knew it, but also we might

---

[1]   The term 'relevation' is borrowed from physicist David Bohm. It would suggest the process of implicate, or potential, forms becoming relevant to explicate, or manifest, conditions and therefore unfolding themselves into the explicate order.

choose to be catalysts, saviours of the World-Soul who would quicken it towards its destiny. This much had the angels revealed, that the cosmic endgame of all worlds and all beings was, and continues to be, the reunion of God within Himself. And, in order that this destiny fulfil itself, the total Original Potential of the Creator must be made actual and everything unique should be made known.

Therefore, the true servant of God shall fix himself upon the revelation of Original Ideas, such as have never before entered the minds of men, yet have existed in the mind of God since before the warring heavens were created. And what the Lord may think, man might make manifest for the benefit of all Creation. We might make manifest a culture of ideas; bring into alliance the worlds of the angels and devils through the actions of our bodies, the craft of our hands and the words of our tongues. For all are material, and rightly the concern of the beings of the plane of Mundus. And whilst the angels and devils bide in us, and do battle amongst themselves to advance the Transcendent Evolutionary Process, it shall be our duty to voice them in harmony, for both, and all, are of the Creator and must be reunited in Him.

(Yet men of the present age have lost the taste for the mana of heaven, and do not consume it though it may fall upon their tongues!)

And then the devils of Gehenna said to Garzibald, "Strive with all your might to become greater. For greatness is the Will of the Creator. And man is not man only, but also Him. So too of God are the devils and the angels—likewise, the thick-headed ox! Though He might use his thick head to break through walls and so discover the entirety of Himself for the life and sake of all that dwells in His body." Thereby, Garzibald learned that the cosmic vocation of man, who was God, was to be creator and explorer of worlds. So he left Gehenna, and drove his flock into the east to learn the language of the Magi of the Orient. Having learned to speak as they did, he became one of them.

Though he had heard of the nature of the World-Soul, not until then had he experienced it—that he, himself, was nothing, and also was God. The angels showed him the former, the devils the latter. The magi then showed him the Way of the Marriage of Opposites, that he might become a prophet for the ages. Having so become, he drove west to Gehenna, that he might share his message with his people. Once he had returned to his homeland, Garzibald gathered together his friends and his foes. All stood around in great anticipation, for they knew that Garzibald had travelled far into the east and might bring knowledge by which they would profit in the here or hereafter. Yet he told them that they had not been born, and would not die, and that the purpose of their lives was to become unique.

Friend and foe alike then laughed at him, proclaiming, "Our purpose is fulfilled! For who amongst us is not unique by virtue of our own names? Who amongst us did not spring from our mothers' wombs, and who has lived whose life has not come to an end?" The people then dispersed, and returned to their homes, and paid no heed to the prophecy of Garzibald. When the devils of Gehenna heard of this, their hearts burned with righteous rage, and they sought to rebuke the fools of the vale, who had since lost their taste for the mana of God, and so no longer dreamed dreams or had visions.

Now, in order that they might show themselves to men without eyes to see, they opened a chasm in the earth, from which echoed their fiery hearts, and flames billowed forth, as though a great ashen cloud, from which the people of Gehenna ran in terror. Only Garzibald remained, who wept for their souls, which breathed not fire but only arid wind. They fled, they fled from Gehenna, and called it by the name of 'hell-on-earth,' yet Garzibald remained and was consumed by the cloud of righteous flame, for he too burned as did the devils and looked with fiery eyes upon the blind. And, though he was consumed, he did not perish, for he knew that he had not been born, and therefore could not die, but would return to the Godhead whence he came. Yet still does the fire of Garzibald echo through the hells, and is apparated on the tongues of wise devils who chance to speak with men on the open fields of Gehenna by moonlight.

On the Fixed Stars

The Zoroastrian angelology of Henri Corbin, depicted in 'Cyclical Time & Ismaili Gnosis,' would suggest that as the five corporeal senses direct the body through the dimension of space, the apparatus of associative thought—which Gurdjieff called the "formatory apparatus"—directs the evolving soul through the dimension of time. Therefore, one who thinks incorrectly moves through time as though by a faulty compass, just as one whose corporeal senses are faulty moves through space with misdirection of body. So, in mind as in body, one who thinks incorrectly risks becoming lost and arriving at unfavourable destinations; trapped within cycles of endless hyparchic recurrence[2].

What is meant by incorrect thinking? The answer to this seemingly profound and epistemologically fraught question is, in actual fact, very straightforward. One thinks incorrectly whose subjectivity prevents him

---

[2]   See volume 1 of J.G. Bennett's *'The Dramatic Universe'* for a full explanation of the concept of Hyparxis. In brief, it is a dimension of cyclical recurrence, through which time and eternity are (potentially) reconciled. It is also, however, the seat of internal fixations of such gravity that the human spirit may be drawn to them and lose all sense of its objective destiny.

or her from considering fully—or even perceiving—the data at hand. As such, one becomes blind to their own biases and is consequently 'free' to act against reason without the intervention of conscience. From the outset, we must consider the nature of conscience. What we may observe, initially, to be an instrument for the detection of 'right' and 'wrong,' more detailed investigation reveals to be a kind of psychical 'tongue,' which is judge in all matters of taste. Taste, of course, is what allows us to distinguish poisons from nutriment. As such, objective taste—which is conscience, in its broadest sense—is the key to orthogenic well-being. Moreover, this correspondence implies that there must exist correct and incorrect modes of thought with respect to the salubrious evolution of the mind towards its destiny. By all accounts, the destiny of this "formatory apparatus" is its transformation into soul-hood. Elsewise, it has no destiny at all. As such, we must conclude that the mind's progress towards its destiny is facilitated by its organ of taste, just as a caterpillar's journey to the chrysalis is made possible by its innate capacity to know which foods it must eat.

After much consideration, it shall become clear that the 'foods' the human psyche must consume in order to arrive at its destiny are Truth and Beauty. These, also, are the primary attributes of God, who is called the Bread of Life for good reason. Thus the mind, knowing Truth and Beauty in abundance, knows its God, and thereby is transformed into a soul. There is no simpler, or more widely conciliated, mystical teaching in existence: Truth and Beauty are, and are the emanations of, God, which our conscience urges us towards, in order that we may fulfil our destiny. So, as a caterpillar to its leaf, must we digest the substances of Truth and Beauty, in order that they marry within us; become the very substance of our minds, and thereby metamorphose it entirely. For, only in this metamorphosed state will the soul be capable of entering into proximity to God. This plane of ethical and aesthetic objectivity, elsewhere called Heaven or Paradise, the 10th century Arabic cosmologist al-Farabi (and Corbin after him) called the sphere of the Fixed Stars.

Meanwhile, the mind's sense of being aids its aspiration towards the Fixed Stars through the attribution of importance to particular concepts, images and mental formations (which shall, hereafter, simply be called 'Thoughts'). When importance is placed upon a Thought, because one has conceived it to be real, the spirit moves through time in a particular direction accordingly[3]—hence allusion is made to the Buddhist metaphors of "crossing the stream," and arriving upon "the far shore." However, rather than aiding the aspiratory evolution of mind, certain Thoughts or—more precisely—sequential patterns of Thought induce its devolution instead. Such patterns of Thought are consequent to the functioning of 'parasites' and 'poisons' which distort the psyche when consumed, causing the misperception of reality in what is, in fact, unreal. So is the importance of taste stressed even further: it is not enough to imbibe what is healthy, but one must also learn to reject what is not. Such afflictions trap the human spirit within time and his being, if he has one, in the hyparchic past.

Lost within the currents of time, he shall forever fall short of his destiny. Yet if, as the great spiritual Ways of antiquity teach, the mind has the potential of evolving beyond time altogether, and thereby becoming eternal—which is to say, if it has the potential of becoming a soul—then there is implied to exist a Way, or numerous Ways, each given form through sequential patterns

---

[3]   Attributed importance is the psychological equivalent of *gravity*. This is intuitively expressed by our assertion that matters of great importance are *grave*. It is, moreover, the principal force which generates and sustains *movement*, be it physical or psychological.

of Thought, which potentiate and scaffold the evolving mind's movement through time towards its destiny: eternity[4].

To further illustrate this point, we may speculate the following: if complexity yields an increase in velocity, a fact observable in modern city life, an organism of near-infinite complexity, such as Homo sapiens, might be said to approach the speed of light. The speed to which we refer is not 186,000 miles per second, but a degree of hyparchic, or psychological, velocity which affords acceleration into the future. Thus the complex mind is capable of perceiving not the finite events, but the orthogenic form of a distant future which culminates, in every case, in the ubiquity of warm and enveloping light. As the mind continues to evolve in this way, and sees ever farther into the future, hyparchic time slows and eventually stops, culminating in the reality of 'eternal life.' Indeed, the properties of an object travelling at the speed of light (insofar as it may still be called an 'object') and those of Nirvana map very well onto each other.

---

[4]   n.b. The evolution of mind beyond time implies, likewise, its necessary transcendence of thought.   For thought, as Gurdjieff suggests, is merely an instrument for the formation of soul.

But one is unlikely to arrive at the Ultimate in a single bound. There are levels through which one must pass before proceeding to the next, as indicated by Ouspensky's 'The Psychology of Man's Possible Evolution.' Each of these accords with a level of being, which evokes a particular pattern of Thought. The Buddha spoke of mundane and supramundane understandings—often these were very different from each other—in order that one might pass through the mundane and arrive at the supramundane.

This is the case with all great spiritual teachers, though it is particularly evident within the writings of G. I. Gurdjieff. For one must first grasp what he is saying, then go beyond it. When one goes beyond it, however, one finds that one's teacher is still by one's side. Though his words have remained the same syntactically, one now notices new semantic patterns emerging in his erudite thoughtscape. This is education in the original sense: the manifestation within oneself of a latent potential for the perception of higher-level truths. Thereby, one discovers that higher-level patterns of Thought—or fixed constellations, if you will— had existed all along, yet had remained invisible to the student who had hitherto operated solely within lower-level patterns of

Thought on account of the level of his being. One might argue, therefore, that there exists only one Way through time—that Way which leads to eternity—but many sequential patterns of Thought which correspond with particular stages of the mind's evolution. All religious teachings of merit disclose this Way, semantically, yet do so via syntactically different patterns of thought at every stage, thereby giving the impression of numerous 'Ways.' For it is written in the Bhagavad Gita 4:11: "However men approach me, even so do I accept them; for the paths at all sides are mine."

Yet, irrespective of the path one chooses, the question remains as to how one might make the conceptual leap from a lower-level pattern of Thought (indicative of a lower level of being) to a higher-level pattern of Thought (indicative of a higher level of being), and to prevent the opposite from occurring. One's approach, in that regard, may be tempered by the teachings of Zoroaster, wherein one is advised that in all patterns of Thought which are neither psychopathically false (Druj) nor transcendentally true (Asha) there exists the potential for the manifestation of forces both of Life and anti-Life. The forces of Life, however, are not wont to dip into the realm of the truly psychopathic, whilst the forces of anti-Life remain forever unable to reach into the realm of the transcendent. For, upon these far extremes, the seemingly ubiquitous admixture of Truth and Falsehood is distilled. Indeed, one may view the process of life's evolution as a kind of orthogenic distillation, whereby spirit and matter are increasingly rarefied.

Yet, within the grand thoughtscape which separates eternity from temporal madness, the forces of Life, which are none other than the Fixed Stars, exist as sources of help which inspire the evolving soul to achieve and operate upon sequentially higher-level patterns of Thought (towards eternity), whilst the forces of anti-Life exist as sources of hindrance which would drag the evolving soul down to lower-level patterns of Thought (towards psychopathy, or moral insanity). Authentic understanding—a process of spirit—may therefore be defined as the discernment of Life from anti-Life with respect to the pattern of Thought wherein one presently operates.

We may reason, consequently, due to the fact that the evolving soul moves through Time via the placement of importance upon particular elements within a pattern of Thought, that Life and anti-Life are implicit within all ordinary patterns of Thought yet become manifest only through the application of importance thereto. As such, valuation is seen to be a process of distillation. In this regard, it may be useful to look to David Bohm's conceptions of implicate and explicate orders, wherein the unfoldment (or becoming explicate) of previously implicate phenomena is a function of their relevation (or becoming relevant). Let us imagine that the Fourth Way system, for instance, is a perfect teaching, infinite and whole in its quintessence—yet that its unfoldment is partial, as dictated by our subjective relevation of elements within said system.

There remains, therefore, the possibility of misusing such a beneficent system to relevate the forces of anti-Life inherent in one's own habitual pattern of Thought by sequentially attributing importance to particular syntactic patterns within the text at hand. Historically, this possibility has been unfolded to devastating effect via the subjective relevation of nearly every holy text known to Man. Yet such relevations—or interpretations, one might say—remain subjective and consequently say nothing, in an objective sense, about the level of being and pattern of Thought wherein the author, himself, was operating. Thus the interpretation reflects the interpreter, and not the author—for its unfoldment is informed by the interpreter's subjective relevation. Therefore, one may apply to the teachings of Gurdjieff, or any spiritual master past or present, the words of the Taoist prophet, Lao Tzu:

> *"My teachings are easy to understand*
> *and easy to put into practice.*
> *Yet your intellect will never grasp them,*
> *and if you try to practice them, you'll fail.*
> *My teachings are older than the world.*
> *How can you grasp their meaning?*
> *If you want to know me,*
> *Look inside your heart."*

One then comes to understand that the evolution of the human mind is directed not by one's adherence to the teachings of this guru or that, or this interpretation or that, but by one's own values (i.e. those elements within a pattern of Thought upon which one places importance). Those who value correctly, submitting to the principles of Thought set forth by the Fixed Stars, are thereby elevated to great ethical heights, whereas those who value incorrectly—the habitual practice of which one might diagnose as a kind of 'value sickness'—descend ultimately into psychopathy, or moral insanity.

Thus, like Jesus of Nazareth, we, too, must learn the art of distillation; to separate the sheep from the goats in order that we might see the unfoldment of the forces of Life, whilst allowing the forces of anti-Life to remain implicate in time. For indeed, when the brother of Teresa of Avila inquired how best to meditate upon hell, she instructed him not to do so at all. And when Rabia al-Basri was asked whether she hated the devil, she replied that she did not have time to hate the devil—too consuming was her love for Allah. According to this mode of reasoning, it becomes apparent that the discernment of values on an objective level—at the level of the Fixed Stars—is imperative to the ongoing evolution of mankind. For our relativistic society abides in a thoughtscape of absolute complexity through which it navigates without a compass! There is hope, however, that the compass of Man might emerge and point northwards again—that we might pass through the Narrow Gate into eternal Life— and that hope is the awakening of Conscience.

In order that one's Conscience be awakened, however, it is often necessary to Work; to oppose actively the inertia of habit for the purpose of permitting the functioning of Higher Intelligences to predominate over the functioning of Lower Intelligences within the mind of Man. What follows, therefore, is an effort to reveal and invoke the spirit of the Natural Imagination; a prism for the numen of starlight.   Thereby,   the   Cosmic Intelligences, and the Fixed Stars to which they are related, might be revealed to human consciousness and objective valuations be made in consequence. For there exists in some artists and prophets the inborn capacity to weave an enlightening 'veil' of Natural Imagination over this invisible world, and thereby make it visible to themselves— and, possibly, to others of like mind.

The cultivation and refinement of the Natural Imagination is the product of the prompting of conscience for the benefit of all who might see it—and, indeed, see beyond it into the sphere of Fixed Stars it serves to clothe. Such Beings exist in all hearts, but the veil through which they are known must be created anew in each new generation; in each individual who strives to know her spiritual vocation. Yet there exist in Man but two truly Fixed Stars, namely, Truth and Beauty, which are the sole inspirations of all authentic philosophy and art, ethics and aesthetics. These two are characterised, respectively, in Man by conscience and innocence, without which no spiritual progress could ever be possible.

Truth corresponds, at its essence, to Man's will, and Beauty to his very mode of being. So are they eternally entwined in our experience, each pointing to its cosmic counterpart. From their union is born Love, the highest of virtues, whereby duality becomes Trinity—and also Wholeness, the manifest expression of God's nature. It shall be our goal, therefore, to approach Truth and Beauty as one; as lovers who've become 'one flesh' through the sacraments of marriage, so that we may draw nearer to Him, our origin and destiny.

On the Naturalistic Science

The Naturalistic Science is the principal means whereby the Natural Imagination might be opened by Men and Women of the present age, such that Truth and Beauty might be known. It is a science in dialogue with Nature; it does not take, but only receives as Nature wills. So it is a listening science, descriptive, evocative and cartographic in its methods, which continually inquires "What is Nature showing me and telling me?" It is a scientific position wherein Nature is the teacher and the scientist its pupil and admirer.

None shall be declared superior to any other in the practice of the naturalistic science—for all who practice are brothers in the art, and their measure of success is their commitment. All that one must concern themselves with is the diligence of their own practice, for it is as much an exercise of Virtue as of science. The very Angel Architects, whose overseer I designate 'Harmonia,' who is the cosmic reconciling

Power[5], awaits him through the message Nature brings.

It tells him that he must remain impartial, for through impartiality is revealed the Trinity in every being. He gazes upon the outermost face of the world, and from this face infers a layered interior. And this is called a 'naturalistic science' because it is the science Nature intended: a science in service of the complete revelation of beings; of the protection, celebration and sanctification of Nature-in-God.

Ordinary science looks upon the outermost face of Nature and proclaims it to be its only face. Then, attempting to manipulate Nature for selfish gain, as the outermost face would afford, burns the bridge of himself and divorces Harmonia from Time. When Man extracts himself from the Natural Order, and benefits at the expense of other beings, he annihilates his only hope of observing his Creator in Nature. Therefore, the first principle of a naturalistic science is the re-integration of the scientist into the Natural Order whence he came. He

---

[5]   The reconciling principle stands in association with the cosmic affirming and negating principles in the philosophy of Gurdjieff. It is the sole peaceful solution to the necessary yet intractable spiritual war brought about by the latter's duality.

must return himself to Nature—and remember his Innocence—in order that he might see Nature for what it is and thereby fulfill his duty towards it.

A Man who is to pursue this science must remember that he, alone, is the measuring instrument. Thus he may, if he desires, plant a stake of arbitrary length into the ground, marking the position from which he shall begin to map the heavens; he may draw a circle, divide it into quarters and, using a series of further lines, each equidistant from its partners, protract the celestial lights by height and distance. Having, with diligent labour, mapped those heavens which are visible to the eye, he may begin to map the earth according to those terms which suit his tastes. Yet it is with the aid of the compass, that most-auspicious instrument of Man which is the universal symbol of his Conscience, that the naturalistic scientist shall see the earth and heavens in alignment.

Imagine, then, how he might also map time and its contents: all plant and animal Life rising and waning on the earth as seasons pass. So Nature reveals a cyclical, habitual pulse: the systole and diastole of Life. In all of this, he asks, "What is Nature revealing?" Let us assume that there exists a message in Her, and we are to read it in full. We shall not read of it in books, but shall know it through the practice of our science. Let us imagine a universal form of process: a unitary message inherent in all movements of Nature. It is of little use to know it second hand—rather, it must be seen and known with those instruments Nature gave us, for Life alone knows Life in all its aspects.

Experience must take place within the soul. One's cartography must be equally a hymn of praise; it must be science but art also, a worthy gift to the beings of Nature whose will to be known have inspired the highest impulses of humanity. For one may read of distant lands and of the species living there, but he alone must be the world's authority in those which live right under his nose. The ravens, the beech trees, the deer must be his family. So, too, must he know his own mind, which is closer to him than all else. The naturalistic scientist must be present absolutely for Nature—his own nature included—for in its ebb and flow it speaks to him.

Though Nature should behave according to habit, the naturalistic science may hardly be practiced as a habitual form of mentation. The naturalistic scientist must be forever alert to novelty, beauty, nobility and purpose. He must see the wisdom in Life and Death, and chronicle that wisdom in detail.

For whoever sees in the Animal Kingdom the adumbration of the Virtues of Eternity fulfils the vocation of humanity; he has become a bridge, a transformer of the Earth within his soul. And he must see this with his own eyes. Therefore, naturalistic science must never become a profession, lest the scientist come to see profit in place of Nature's message. He must practice this brotherly art with selflessness—absolute selflessness. Indeed, he might go so far as to let no one know that he is a naturalistic scientist—a practitioner of the Way of the Natural Imagination—until he is on his deathbed[6].

He might practice his science alone or with a single close companion for whom he would gladly give his life. For that which is called a 'naturalistic science,' or even a 'brotherly art,' is in truth a deep religion of Conscience and Beauty. It is a Way through which a human being integrates his body, soul and intellect into Life's fabric with consciousness. It is a Way generative of a New Heaven and a New Earth—for the

---

[6]   The benefits of self-concealment and seamless integration suggested by Naturalistic Science are likewise cornerstones of the Islamic Malamatiyya, or People of Blame. This practice is noted for its capacity to guard the soul against egoistic corruptions which would undermine the true purpose of the spiritual work.

naturalistic scientist's methods are both cartographic and prayerful in nature. Nature, itself, is offered respect by admitting its individuality and being. The naturalistic scientist creates laudatory maps of heaven and earth, engaging intellect, feeling and action.

In the practice of the naturalistic science, one takes it upon himself to formulate a map of the entirety of his own experience—most especially of his experience of the Fixed Stars—and also to map the experiences of those persons who have ventured farther afield, as a preparatory measure for a journey one desires to one day take. For cartography is the rightful business of explorers, firstly as a means of orientation within a novel environment (for even the familiar is novel to one who truly looks for the first time) and secondly as a guidebook for future explorers—for future colonists of nascent worlds.

Through his cartographic efforts, he seeks out the hidden Fixed Stars—those agencies whose form of process is isomorphic between all possible dimensions of being. There is no way of identifying such a thing, or Intelligence, except by comparison across dimensions. This is not to suggest interdisciplinary research, merely, but the simultaneous cartographic exposition of natural, imaginal, and ideal phenomena with the aim of arriving at a unitary worldview through recourse to multi-dimensional being-processes. In other words—a workable world-map which encompasses the terrestrial, celestial, psychic and intellectual; a *unus mundus* to orientate the human soul in flux.

That which we shall call herein 'Harmonia,' which is the proper name of cosmic beauty, pertains to and is equally applicable conceptually within each of the aforementioned dimensions; is a guiding principle, in collaboration with the North Star of Conscience, which offers objectively applicable support to all beings, and in every dimension of their manifold existences. We need, furthermore, a reliable means of distinguishing between the indications of the Fixed Stars and those chimerical phenomena—given morals and ideas of beauty—which are roughly like in appearance to the Fixed Stars but are in fact distractions or hindrances which delude the traveler and set him off that course his Nature has intended him to take.

Having become fluent in the language of such a cartography, one gradually develops the ability to translate freely between the dimensions of experience, and to observe the unitary quality of the Fixed Stars in all experience. So he must establish, in the first instance, rather than a mere amalgamation of data arising out of the natural world, a sound spiritual orientation through which to approach such data as they arise. Thereby, it is gradually understood that the world of things (the 'exterior' of beings, or Res) is not wholly distinct from the world of psyche (the 'interior' of beings, or Anima) and neither are they related as might be an object and its mirror, but by a unitary origin of mutual correspondence (the 'transcendence' in beings, or Intellectu). Indeed, each world has its own manner of relative independence, but is simultaneously bound into a *unus mundus* via its common interactions with the seamlessly multi-dimensional Fixed Stars, which are properly 'located' within the divine Intellect which is within, and is the Rational Mind of, God.

One might imagine, for lack of a better analogy, that a single sheet of paper, which is 'one-dimensional' in itself, is at several places folded like origami to yield three, or even four, dimensions, which are rendered observable only through the action of the fold. So, too, is our universe extended and related by the very folding of time-space, which is the consequence of the Presence of Cosmic Beings. Thus, whatever is of three or more dimensions might be said to possess a life of its own, whereas that which appears to be of one dimension only, or even two—a flat surface comprising only inner and outer aspects—is a 'blind spot' whereby an insufficient cartography has failed to draw one face of a phenomenon into association with its fellows, via the Fixed Stars, through which all things are extended and related.

So it is understood that knowledge of the Fixed Stars is required in order that any naturalistic science be granted a meaningful point of embarkation. In short, it is the fact of our beginning with the Fixed Stars, in the manner of a uniquely top-down approach to the natural world, which distinguishes the naturalistic science from traditional scientific endeavours. Indeed, its methodologies are drawn from the positioning of the Fixed Stars as the primary points of departure—for only through their prevenient grace might the Natural Imagination of Man be opened.

In so doing, one aims to create a science which functions within three dimensions simultaneously. It is not intended to be a 'trans-' or 'meta-' science, but instead a thoroughly penetrative one, wherein the entire essence of phenomena are considered. It is not to be an abstract science, divorced from the senses of Man, but instead one which engages deeply with his senses, his psyche, and his intellect. It is a re-integrative science, an opponent of the alienation of Man from the Natural Order.

Thus the Fixed Stars, which are the cornerstone of its exposition, are best conveyed in accordance with their characteristically human faces, and not through the abstract terminology which might otherwise have been used to describe these cosmic principles. For, as they move upwards along the biological chain, from single cells to complete human organisms, their cosmic potentialities are further and further explicated in all their richness of character. Indeed, it is precisely this richness of character which is manifested to greater and greater degrees as the evolutionary process progresses.

At lower levels of complexity, one is able to refer only to basic forms of animism: to controller, transcriber, messenger, etc. But at progressively higher levels of order and complexity they cannot be adequately characterised as 'principles' or 'forces' only, because these terms do not carry in themselves enough vitality—enough personality, even—to fully convey their operations at the level of the human organism. Of course, these entities are not human—they are more than human, but in explicating themselves through humanity; in shaping human souls to a greater or lesser extent, they may be related to most intimately precisely through those human souls who have submitted most completely to their grace. For this reason, the Naturalistic Science must include a thorough study of the lives of great saints and mystics, which reveal to us most clearly, and in richest detail, the evolutionary intelligences at work in the natural order[7].

---

[7]   One may also consider them to be, in accordance with a view for psychology, to be references in aid of establishing the parameters of ideal mental health, without which the goals of psychology are forever fraught with subjectivism.

Clear-Eyed Creatures, All

———————————

What heav'n—
       but that which joyful creatures show?
Their bliss, by bright and clearest eyes revealed,
Is truth which only innocence may know;
Is love, which Midnight's cloak cannot conceal.
Whispered voices, warmly cadenced song,
Speak of springtime peeking through the snow;
She lauds the verdant saplings, growing strong;
Full life-limbs which the flashing sun bestows.
And then Our Star recedes towards his home
Within the Earth's soft, steadfast womb wherein
Sweet succor lies; Night's allies wake and roam
The meadowlands, by moonlight free from sin.
Clear-eyed creatures all, each night and day,
Speak joyful creeds, their Maker's holy Way.

On the Great Ways

I

A man or woman of sincere intent
must either find within herself the innate
capacity to interpret the Divine Meaning of
one of the existing Great Ways, which are the
ancient religions of Conscience, or she must
receive revelation of her own Way via the
opening of the Natural Imagination[8], through
which Truth and Beauty are made known.
For it is written in the Upanishads, "However
men approach me, even so do I accept them,
for the paths at all sides are mine." Thus all
Ways are commissioned by God, whose
essence is Truth, and crafted by the Archangel
Harmonia, whose essence is Beauty,
according to His prescient instruction.

Now the Son of God is called Love,
whose visible aspect is Light. And it is true
that no one goes to the Father except
through Him; that He became Man in order
that all sin, which is the consequence of the
predominance of the Lower Intelligences over
the Higher Intelligences, might be vanquished

---

[8] This term shall designate, throughout, the ability
to intuit correspondences between the psychic and material
planes, whereby is potentially revealed a transcendent,
universal form of process.

from the Kingdom of Heaven. Meanwhile the Archangel Harmonia, who is the Handmaiden of God, and chief architect among the Higher Intelligences, has shaped all Ways which lead from this world to the next.

Though she is glorious, it was commanded by her in the Book of Revelations that all glory be to God; that none should pray to her, or bow before her. Yet even the holy dimensions of Res, Anima and Intellectu she has united at the instruction of her Lord. In order that Man, himself, might pass from Res to Anima, and from Anima to Intellectu—which is the greatest of all passages, the Via Dei—she has crafted a bridge, even as she, herself, remains behind. It is by this bridge, too, that God shall come to reunite himself within Himself and so receive, for others' sake, His own Destiny: His One True Desire, for the benefit of all sentient beings. This bridge, which is placed into the heart of Man—who is made in the image of God—in the form of an organ of augury, the Natural Imagination, has been constructed by Harmonia in its foundations, yet in order that this Inspired Way might be warded against infiltration by the Lower Intelligences, as a virus to the nucleus of Life, it must be co-created by Men and Women who have first excluded from their hearts all trace of the influence of said Lower

Intelligences, which are becoming of neither human nor animal life.

II

The likeness of this Most-Holy Bridge has been called Vision, or the Natural Imagination, and is opened through sincere submission to the voice of Conscience, who is the High Counsellor of the Creator, and is of His Being, with supreme regard for whose "orienting influence" He has created all worlds and all beings therein. Yet Man has come also under the influence of the Oppressor, who is the Enemy of the Creator, who has attempted to become God, himself, and thereby to purloin his Maker's Destiny. In so doing, he burns all bridges, for Harmonia has placed a 'spell' upon her sacral craftsmanship such that any being amongst the Lower Intelligences who should attempt to cross causes its instantaneous conflagration. So he creates fragmentation and isolation, even in the midst of harmony personified.

It is the work of all Men and Women of sincere intent to permit Harmonia to work within their psyche, such that bridges once burnt might be re-built; that she who has followed Man into Time—for the benefit of God's created children—might enter, once again, into Eternity. For it is Harmonia who would build the bridge from Innocence to experience, and the Iron Beast, who is revealed to us through Automatic Subjective Compulsion, who would sabotage her work— or, rather, it is she who would sabotage it, for the sake of Our Cosmos! Indeed, such a safeguard is necessary, for the kingdom of heaven is besieged even now by violent Powers who would seize them by force[9].

Only by the deconstruction of Automatic Subjective Compulsion is Harmonia permitted to build, because that bridge which the Iron Beast crosses is the ruin of all. This 'Sacred Quarantine,' as though from a virus of spirit, is at work in all worlds, and is the obstacle of all Men and Women who contain within their minds the influence of the Lower Intelligences. Yet, for whoever is liberated from their influence is crafted by Harmonia, at the instruction of her Father Creator, a Royal Road to the True Desire, which is of God, and is our prevenient Destiny to inherit.

Such is the most-sacrosanct terminus of every Great Way of antiquity, given to us

---

[9]   Matthew 11:12: "And from the days of John the Baptist until now the kingdom of heaven suffers violence, and the violent take it by force."

by our forefathers, and of every individual
Way foreseen by the Natural Imagination in
the present age.

On the Quaternity

I

Quaternity, the quality of wholeness derived from a relationship comprising four sequentially recurring entities, is a form of process uniquely affecting the cosmos' biological dimension. It is the means by which perishable organisms, which lack the sentience to act consciously in accordance with virtue, whereby is revealed the Godhead's trinity, are related to and partake of their origin and destiny. Through cyclical repetition, temporally limited beings imprint themselves upon eternity, and thus become integrated into it.

We experience directly the effects of quaternal processes through the archetypes of the collective unconscious, whereby the psychical tendencies of our forefathers manifest in us, and in Lamarckian evolution of all kinds. Notwithstanding, the procession of the seasons, and life's robust responses to their passage, are the clearest examples of the quaternal form of process on Earth, through which even basic life-forms are immortalized. So it is the case, on our planet, that the perpetuation of life beyond a single lifetime requires the Quaternity's grace. And, by understanding the essence of the seasons, in terms of their form of process, one may recognize an isomorphic process within the psyche, which our lifestyles may facilitate or inhibit, such that our potential integration with eternity is reinforced or left to wash away.

As such, the Natural Imagination intuits a correspondence between the procession of day and night, and the birth and death of the manifest cosmos. So, too, exists an intermediary level of correspondence between the progress of a single day and the year's four seasons. Our habitual tendency to divide these cyclical phenomena into four interrelated parts is evident in each case: morning, afternoon, evening and night; infancy, youth, maturity, old age; spring, summer, autumn, winter; etc. The *purpose* of so dividing our lives, though far from our everyday consciousness, is to imprint our legacies into eternity.

II

Trapped within the confines of linear time, the soul of man is destined to wither and wane. Indeed, the linear quality of time is of an inhibitory nature, and so places limitations on an otherwise infinite spirit. Limitation, however, is the price we pay for manifestation. In order, then, to reconcile the qualities of the infinite spirit, existing within eternity, and the finite mind-body amalgam, existing within time, we must appeal to what J. G. Bennett called Hyparxis, which is the domain of cyclical recurrence. The procession of seasons is one such appeal, whereby life on earth perpetuates.

It is easy to imagine that the seasons occur automatically, on accident, having their origin in haphazard planetary mechanics. Such a belief will lead us, also, to the conclusion that the psychic correspondence to the seasons, being indicative of a universal form of process, must occur automatically, without conscious intervention. This, it appears, would be an error. Indeed, left to their own devices, very few persons would prove able to recognise and manifest within their psyches the form of process which governs the terrestrial seasons.

Rather, by careful deliberations and efforts, it may be possible to shape one's lifestyle around this cosmic form of process, enabling harmonization with it. Consequently, one's own psychic energies may be amplified. This, it seems, might well prove salubrious when applied to the modern malaise of exhaustion. To live by one's own energies, without the support of cosmic processes, is to live a lesser life than one is capable of. Indeed, we all require such supports; and the greatness of man is determined by the extent of his harmonization with processes which are greater than himself.

We may imagine, then, that the entire living soul is known in the procession of the seasons. As they are earth's vessel for the furtherance of life, so is the soul the psyche's vessel for the furtherance of the life within itself. Moreover, each season finds predominance at a different stage of life, and at different times of day and night. They are known in the opus of the alchemists, and in the cosmic quaternity. Indeed, they constitute, collectively, the telos of all life within our universe; are the guiding lights of all living beings; are angels of purpose and meaning.

Spring is the season of youth; the first season. It is characterised by spontaneous play, and defined by the free energies of Joy. The proper function of the spring within the human spirit is the inspiration of vision. Now, a person may begin to develop a sense of life's meaning and purpose, even if he does not, or cannot, understand it intellectually. He may see, within his soul, the reason for his manifestation, and the end-game of his spiritual destiny.

The spring of life concludes, and its summer begins, when one's purposeful vision is complete. Now is the season of resolve; the second season. And none may possess the proper resolve who have not known the vision of spring, which lives on as the fuel of the summer. No longer does one want for inspiration, but action. One knows what is required, and pursues it. Thus, the summer of the soul is characterised by conscious striving, and defined by the energy of love. So is the summer a season of continuous action in pursuit of a divine goal, pre-cognized in the springtime of life.

Autumn, then, presents itself as a time of fruition. Its arrival is heralded by the realization of the goal, and the ecstasy of knowing completion. What one imagines in spring, and pursues in summer, autumn fulfils. Now, one may relish in the fruits of the harvest, and enjoy thoroughly the product of their labours. The purpose of life is fulfilled, its task completed. Life has achieved maturation, ripeness, and offers itself up to be enjoyed. One has not, however, fully realised its deepest mystery.

For, until winter, one may not recognize the most-holy sunset, that time of perfect rest and submission. Indeed, winter bears much similitude with spring; is an anticipation of spring, in fact; a readying oneself for a new day's dawning. Thus, winter is a time for contemplation, for the fruits of this life are fleeting, and death shall strip them away. One may listen for echoes, however, of the eternal in his actions hereto. He must arrive at the assured knowledge that God is with him, and banish all fear from his heart. He must become, as he was in youth, his essential self; yet he shall find, after autumn, that his essence, now, is greater than before, and filled with the spirit of wisdom. Only then is he ready to die, and greet the New Spring with open arms.

Recall, too, that a lesser simulacrum of the four seasons is present in a single day, and also in the sexual act, which all serve the furtherance of life. Indeed, the seasons, themselves, are simulacra of the birth and death of the entire cosmos. They are worlds within worlds, born of a universal form of process, which provide to all living beings necessary energies for the beginning, ending and recurrence of each stage of life. So it is the case that one who lives by the seasons lives well, for life that knows the Quaternity is eternal.

On the Trinity

I

Value is inherent in all life as a regulating factor. On the level of lower life forms and automatic processes in man, this value is manifested without consciousness on the part of the manifesting organism. At all levels, value is the accordance with one's own form. So, being corresponds directly with value, since being refers to the ability to be oneself in an environment that is not oneself. In this light, it is clear that the corruption of being, one's own or another's, is likewise a deviation from the norm of value. Disease is de-valuation, and vice versa.

Through this premise, we may infer a force of de-valuation—though, in accordance with its own form, certainly not without value—operating throughout the universe, which strives towards a state of undifferentiated formlessness. The foundation of autonomic values, which is to say, the integrity of being, operating on the organic level determines the capacity for the manifestation of values of consciousness. Where the autonomic values are compromised, conscious values are precluded. This phenomenon, consequent to de-valuing influences on the sub-psychic level, may be called 'sin by deficiency.'

At the level of consciousness, however, an organism becomes responsible for the manifestation of values. The degree of any value is limited exclusively by its corresponding degree of lawfulness. As such, pure value must be absolutely free. Being and value are therefore to be viewed as mutually determining conditions, growing into existence together. Being is energy which, like a river in flow, is always active by nature. Value shapes such energy into 'bodies' which, by virtue of increasing uniqueness, are considered to be of higher level of being, with subsequent access to energies of increasing degrees of freedom.

We have hereto been concerned principally with the material, vital and intellectual energies, which are shaped by value into being and form, collectively, the vertical aspect of the Catholic trinity. There exists moreover a non-linear aspect, arising from the vital core, which directs the orthogenic life-process of all biological beings and may be characterized symbolically as follows:

1) The hope for enlightenment is given from above, through a glimpse of transcendent beauty; the seeker is called to the search.

2) Whilst still in a passive state, the seeker 'takes action' with his senses to realise the goal of the search; the hope from above gestates within him, culminating in a state of submission to the Father-Spirit, which is called faith.

3) The complementary impulses of hope and faith are reconciled through the birth of love; the level of being rises and so transforms the active will and passive function.

Whoever becomes like Mary shall birth the inner Christ: a being which is perfectly true to itself, and so likewise perfect in value. The core of the triad outlined here is its Marial aspect: hope is given, love is to come; faith must be cultivated presently. The antithesis of faith is fear. Fear must be overcome through faith. The essence of faith is receptivity to hope; it is the consequence of the impressions made by hope upon the psyche. Such impressions form in the mind, which is the virginal womb of the soul, the inner body; the interior castle wherein hope and faith are reconciled. So love is like both hope and faith, but is itself in essence.

Or, faith is the capacity to allow hope to work within oneself. Thus, faith is characterised by inner tranquility; a state of inspired consent. Which is to say, tranquility engenders the impulse of faith. So must tranquility be the state of function towards which the seeker must strive. Tranquility, alone, is achieved independently by man: hope is super-human, love is transcendent. Hope foresees the birth of love. Thus, the faith of man must provide for the influx of hope. In this regard, we may imagine that the psyche, itself, is female; it bears the imprint of the cosmic feminine, irrespective of one's physical sex.

Through the study of embryology, we may come to learn much about the psychic processes of engendering the impulse of faith. We must study, especially, the mode of functioning of the pregnant female. Thus our sound knowledge of the biological world may edify our partial insights into the psychic nature. Pregnancy is a time of simultaneous expansion and concentration of energies. A nascent love expands in direct proportion to faith's maturing concentration. The pregnant woman must enter a time of purity, lest the infant be afflicted or stillborn.

Hope for a future love puts all the world to order. Faith allows itself to be shaped as hope wills. Hope is prescience. Faith is a vessel. Love is destiny. So is the greatest among these love, which alone is Real. Now the mystic seeks to cultivate her faith for the sake of love. And she must cultivate her faith by appeal to the image of hope's prescience, which is called the True Desire. All wills turn and unite in service of this: the likeness of God in one's own mind, the Natural Imagination. And the Natural Imagination is rendered vivid in relation to the fullness of one's faith. For, by faith, it is realised.

Calling to mind an image of perfect beauty, which is made perfect in accordance with one's self, the mystic knows herself to be remembering. This is called the memory of Innocence, which is her hyparchic, or recurrent, condition. Where such a condition is plural and irreconcilable, she must allow herself to occupy all hyparchic worlds simultaneously. Doing so causes the awakening of Conscience. Meditating upon hyparchic images, they begin to coalesce and transform under the influence of the nascent Conscience. This is called by Gurdjieff repairing the past. At last, the True Desire is one, and all wills have united as one under the influence of transcendental love. When the New Heaven and the New Earth she clearly sees, then she will know what to do.

Each hyparchic world is an island of will, a partiality whose fulfillment is to the exclusion of another. But whoever sees the New Heaven and New Earth sees beyond hyparxis into eternity. Hyparxis is hell;

eternity is heaven. One must cross over the stream of hyparxis in order to arrive upon the far shore of eternity. To do so requires an act of profound faith. And any act of faith must be made in hope of a future love.

Hope may lead you to hyparxis, but no further.   Now faith must forge itself in conscience, which alone may guide the right coalition of imaginal gods which hope has brought forth from the Natural Imagination. This process J. G. Bennett called the reconstruction of the will.

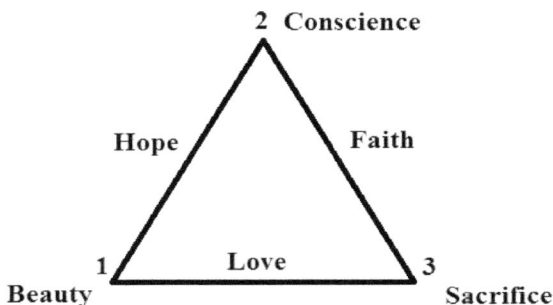

The mystic's journey is initiated through her perception of beauty. Beauty engenders in her the impulse of 'hope-for-a-future-love.' Experiencing simultaneously, on account of the functioning in her of the Lower Intelligences, the desire to devour and be devoured by beauty, the sincere seeker submits her desires to Conscience in their entirety. This engenders the impulse of faith.

By faith, hope is at last set free from the urge to dominate. The act of sacrifice thus engenders the impulse of love. To the lover, beauty returns freely. So is the cycle completed.

Without beauty, there can be no memory of Innocence. Without Conscience, reconstruction of the will could not take place. Without sacrificing one's own will, there would be no room for love in one's heart. The human will must be reconstituted before it can be sacrificed. All is for the sake of the Fixed Stars:

"Beauty is truth, truth beauty,—that is all
Ye know on earth, and all ye need to know."
   - J. Keats

All of the life impulses are engendered by beauty. In the heart of a pure lover, all may be engendered instantly, simultaneously. Beauty is a reflection of a transcendental pattern, which is the origin and fruition of all virtuous striving.

Beauty of mind is more perfect than beauty of body; beauty of spirit is more perfect than beauty of mind. She is called Harmonia who is the Cosmic Soul of Beauty. She is not God, but is the gateway to God: the perfect form who shows the way beyond form.

II

Faith is the power to allow oneself to be shaped by virtue; the capacity to give up fixed notions of self-hood and be whatever the situation requires. That is why it is synonymous with the Universal Receiving Impulse. Hope is the promise of acquiring Individuality; of shaping the world in accordance with one's True Desire. That is why it is synonymous with the Universal Affirming Impulse. Love is the fruit of the union of hope and faith; the transformation of being which occurs when hope and faith lose themselves in each other. Love, therefore, is greater than either hope or faith: it contains both hope and faith, but remains uniquely itself. That is why it is synonymous with the Universal Reconciling Impulse. It is for this reason that we may unreservedly state that God is love: love contains the Trinity within a single impulse.

Hope is purified by conscience; faith is purified by sacrifice. Without beauty, there can be no hope. Without conscience, there can be no faith. Without sacrifice, there can be no love. Therefore, the essence of virtue is conscious sacrifice for the sake of the liberation of beauty from the unmanifest.

Both hope and faith must be informed and directed by Conscience. Without

Conscience, hope is corrupted by the de-valuing influence of the Lower Intelligences and takes the form of acquisitiveness, ambition and greed in all its forms. Faith becomes mass-mindedness, gullibility and the inability to think for oneself. (Capitalism is corrupted hope's domination of corrupted faith). Love, which is the greatest of the three, becomes the will to power. It seeks likewise to corrupt all that is thought to be more beautiful than itself, dragging beauty back into the unmanifest. Thus it reveals itself as jealousy, the absence of beauty. These three may be called anti-hope, anti-faith and anti-love, respectively, because each is directed in its form of process by de-valuing influences. As in the triad of pure life impulses, the negative triad, too, is engendered by the perception of beauty.

III

Beauty, itself, may be categorised as morphic beauty, the beauty emanating from material forms, vital beauty, the beauty emanating from spontaneous life processes, and spiritual beauty, the beauty emanating from the conscious exercise of virtue. The numinous quality of each may be experienced, respectively, as esse in res, esse in anima and esse in intellectu. Each therefore corresponds with a level of being: all persons have a physical presence, but their capacity to exercise virtue shall determine the absence or presence of a vital and intellectual being and its corresponding level.

A poem, in itself, may emanate morphic beauty. A poem read aloud, however, may emanate both morphic and vital beauty; its content may emulate spiritual beauty and evoke it in others. Even a painting or sculpture may evoke vital and spiritual beauty. Each level of emanation bears correspondence with each successive level of being.

However, when the triadic impulses are corrupted, the image of beauty may become distorted with subjectivism, so that 'like' is conflated with beauty and 'dislike' with degenerate form. The pursuit of 'like' and aversion to 'dislike' serves the purpose of entrenching in habit the corrupted life impulses, submitting them to the workings of Automatic Subjective Compulsion, and desensitising the aesthetic sense. In this way, the Cosmic Trinity may be hijacked completely in the human mind by the de-valuing influences, because its capacity for self-regulation is dependent upon the correct functioning of the aesthetic sense and subsequent responsiveness to virtue.

Beauty is most concentrated in its spiritual form, and most diffuse in its morphic form. The evocation of spiritual beauty will bring a sensitive person to tears and trembling. This is the consequence of a sudden and dramatic influx of hope as it acts upon a deeply receptive faith. So may hope be experienced as 'uplifting joy' and faith as 'grounding sorrow.' The effect of the perception of rarefied beauty is to evoke their simultaneous impact within oneself, which is outwardly perceived as tearful trembling. In so doing, they elicit the manifestation of the reconciling impulse, subject to sacrifice, whereby love is conceived and soul created. This is the inner experience of—or participation in—the immaculate conception. It is immaculate not because it is sexually virginal or abstinent, but because it has occurred upon the rarefied heights of the spirit, upon which level of being alone can man be called whole.

This is man's participation in the cosmic sexuality, the eternal pattern of creation. When such a pattern is subject to the laws of the material world, the unity of the pattern descends into multiplicity, but free from material influences the triad's unity is repeatedly reiterated on successively higher levels of being, culminating in the infinite expansion and mutual realisation of the three great primordial cosmic impulses. This infinitude of triadic unity, which is the harmonic destiny of the vital universe, may be called the eternal font of all beauty existing.

Having begun the cosmic process in man—indeed, through but the twinkle in lovers' eyes—the cosmic beauty is at last liberated, once and for all, from the unmanifest, and so concludes what it began, through a distant cry for help. Now love, which contains within itself both hope and faith, is exalted on the altar of beauty. The unfathomable numinosity of the Cosmic Quaternity is complete, for beauty is made more beautiful by the encapsulation of the Trinity therein. It is upon this point that we realise the necessity of a trans-infinite dimension of absolute freedom wherein absolute virtue reigns supreme.

Again, the goal of human existence is the liberation of beauty from the unmanifest.

IV

Let your spirit be like a clear beam of light. Let your soul be like a river of music. Let your body be like a wide, old oak. This is the way of inner harmony. Let no self, but conscience alone, rule the inner life of man. All selves must bow before conscience.

Therefore, turn all decisions over to conscience, and decide but to submit to its word. Conscience resolves all disputes between selves, within and without; it is the master of selves.

The seat of consciousness is but one self of many. The interventions of conscience will set these selves to order if they are heeded. For conscience shows the clear path to unity. Each centre must be independent from its fellows; before a person may become completely himself, his intellectual, emotional and moving centres must be free to experience themselves as distinct wholes. All parts must become spiritualised; which is, penetrated by the light of the spirit. From above, such spiritualisation affects the reason first, the feeling second, and the body third. A single thread must run through, and be known to, all three in order that wholeness might emerge.

To this end, we might imagine the 'continent' of humanity to be shared by not less than three 'nations.' By divine decree, each nation is entitled to its own practices. Thus, never must one nation attempt to justify the oppression of another's religion and culture. However, the nature of humanity is such that, in the ordinary lives of its citizens, only one culture is permitted the expression of its practices at any one time, thus subjugating temporarily the others. There is also the case wherein the habitual tendency of one 'nation' to dominate the 'continent' causes the oppression and eventual extinction of neighbouring cultures. The subordinated cultures will soon turn to insidious and subversive means of expressing their cultural norms, despite the oppressive climate, for the sake of their continuing survival.

So does the peace-loving leader call for a dialogue between all nations for the conscious creation of situations in which all may practice harmoniously their respective religions and express their respective cultures. This 'multi-national' or 'continental' event, called harmonic worship, affords a level of inner-togetherness, or being, which is impossible in the normal course of events wherein each national religion is practiced sequentially, or one dominates and subjugates all others. The discernment of the necessity to make peace between nations and engage in harmonic worship may be likened to the birth of the magnetic centre in man, wherein the needs of a potential whole are placed above the desires of its actual parts. And the most honourable aim leading to the actualisation of unity is the cessation of oppression within oneself and between all selves, within and without.

V

We must consider less our thoughts than the origins of our thoughts. There are certain 'enlightening' ideas, the levation of which lead to moments of self-consciousness, as well as 'obfuscating' ideas, the levation of which lead to moments of, or indeed indefinite, identification. The cause of the levation of either such category is the determining condition of the category itself. The relative balance of the individual's responsiveness to the sources of enlightening and obfuscating ideas determine his level of consciousness.

The exercise of will is man's sole defense against the vortex of obfuscating ideas. Where the will is inactive, consciousness falls into the vortex and may, therein, only be retrieved by the activity upon him of, and his subsequent receptivity to, enlightening ideas. Of himself, man is powerless to escape the vortex. It is a domain of pure identification, wherein 'I' 'do' and 'make' all that is experienced.

Being which has entered the vortex cannot see beyond the vortex itself; one has no consciousness of that which the vortex is not. For this reason, man is fragmented by the vortex and divested of his powers; his will sleeps therein because it believes itself to be

DREAMS OF TRUTH AND BEAUTY

willing the levation of all thoughts and feelings that arise from the abyss of slumber. Again, a man cannot be awakened from the vortex, as from a deep sleep, except by great shock or bright light. But a man who is awakened from sleep by a shock shall, in the absence of light, soon return to his dreams. Thus, in order to awaken and to remain awake, one must come under, and remain under, the influence of enlightening ideas.

Such ideas come from 'above' and call a man towards them; obfuscating ideas come from 'below' and call a man towards them. Enlightening ideas promise the serendipity of individuality; obfuscating ideas promise the acquisition of selfhood. So, the inner struggle of all persons may be summarised as the conflict of decision between acquisition and serendipity; or, of taking with one's material part, versus receiving with one's spiritual part.

Notwithstanding, it is possible that the spirit may become 'materialised' or the body 'spiritualised.' The beginning and end of the materialisation of the will is identification, such that the will becomes gradually subject to the domination of the material self. The beginning of the spiritualisation of the body is its conformity to the rhythms of nature, for the body is of natural origin and must subordinate itself to the Earth in order that the spirit may acquire the necessary power to wield it, though always within those limits honoured by nature, herself, who is subordinated, in turn, to the cosmic environs of the solar system.

And though the body of man is from the Earth, his will is of solar origin. This is why 'enlightenment' is synonymous with exercise of the will, and why it is orthogenic that the body be subordinated to the will as the Earth is subordinated to the sun. Thus it may be said that the will is the sun-part of man, and the body the earth-part. So is the relational dynamic between the earth and the sun isomorphic with the orthogenic relational dynamic between the body and will of man.

The eyes are for receiving the sun into the earth, and so are the material face of the soul, which must mediate between them. As consciousness is the radiation of light from the will, so is the inner face of the soul that which allows consciousness to be received by the body. Though the body ages, the eyes do not age. Whoever has beautiful eyes is beautiful forever. Thus all soul-qualities radiate through the eyes of man, such that they are rightly called 'the windows of the soul,' whilst remaining 'of the soul itself.'

The illumination of the eyes is the consequence of the conjunction of the solar and earthly parts of man, whose subsequent emanations are composed of love, joy, hope, innocence and warmth. The capacity for such emanations is manifested from 'behind' the eyes themselves—via the perception of beauty, which is the prism of sunlight. But whoever has lost themselves within the Vortex cannot perceive beauty, because they cannot see or hear beyond it. Such is the case for the ears also, which are capable of the perception of beauty through the reverberations of the sun's creation's expressions of love, joy, hope, innocence and warmth. (It is not possible, however, to smell, taste or touch beauty through these same prismatic emanations.) Seeing this to be true, the body will rise in service to the sun. None can respect the will of man who are ignorant of its noble origins.

All of nature is of the earth, and responds to the sun, but only man is bestowed with a sun-nature of his own. Of man, the sun is God; indeed, the sun is truly supernatural. He cannot know beyond the sun because the sun-nature is his highest part. It is the right ruler of the life of man, from which his consciousness emanates like light from the sun itself. So has the sun imbued man with its own aspect, and made him in the image of itself. The body of man is given to him by the earth in order that he may realise his sun-nature. For the body must return to the earth, but the gift of the sun-nature is enduring. "I am the kinsman of the sun," the child of God.

The will of man need not be exercised in thought or outward action, but through the will to emanate consciousness. As the earth finds its own way by the energy of the sun, so will the body find its own way by the light of consciousness. So is the struggle of the earth and sun reconciled by the perception of beauty. In all affairs of being, beauty is the arbiter. Beauty is harmony. So must the mystic take beauty with him wherever he goes.

The body must be emptied of compulsions; it must be broken open in order that it might pour. How is the body to be broken open while it yet lives? There is an icy burg around the font of the heart-spring. It must be shattered by beauty, in order that the body might be flooded with light—a light that will banish the shades of compulsion.

VI

The right use of the human body is for the realisation of the sun-nature of his will. When a person is alone, and nothing presses down upon him, his character, or true self, is revealed. This is the natural man, and alone forms the foundation upon which higher, or transformed, man is constructed. So must a man first find serenity before he can aspire to transform.

Man as Solar System

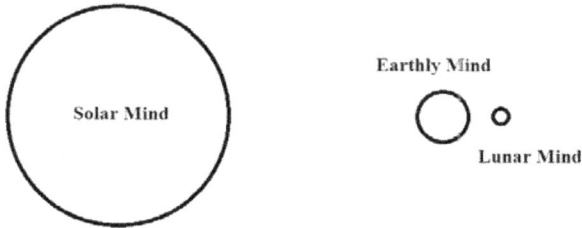

Earthly Mind

Solar Mind

Lunar Mind

Lunar Mind corresponds with the influences of the Lower Intelligences, possessing all their properties, including illusory approximation to the True Desire. This corresponds, in turn, with the ability of the moon to reflect sunlight and so provide a 'false sun' to its viewer. Solar Mind corresponds with the influences of the Higher Intelligences, which are objectively 'enlightening.' Both the Solar Mind and Lunar Mind exert an influence on the true self, or 'Earth Mind,' of Man.

VII

Natural Imagination consists in the progressive realisation of correspondences between natural and cosmic forms, and forms of process, and psychical structures and processes. The observation of such processes implies in natural, cosmic and psychic forms of activity a common source of origin. We may therefore infer that all such correspondent forms of process partake of a unique, transcendent pattern of relationship wherein is found the potential required for the proper ordering of its manifest instances.

In psychical terms, the chief utility of the Natural Imagination as a method of understanding is its ability to allow us to observe directly with the senses psychical forms and processes which, otherwise, can only be discussed as abstract concepts. Through our assumption of a common source of origin of natural, cosmic and psychical phenomena, the psychology of correspondences distinguishes itself from a psychology of symbolism. A correspondence is not a symbol. Rather, it is an observation of two or more morphic or relational dynamics which must necessarily partake in a single form of process due to their common source of origin.

Therefore, all that was previously said concerning the Trinity of Father-Spirit, Mary and Christ may be said also of the sun, earth and life, respectively. These partake in the same transcendent pattern in each case, forming an isomorphic correspondence in their relational dynamic. This triad may subsequently be observed in the sexual act, which, through the impression of male upon female, culminates in the conception of a child which comprises both male and female yet, in its essential constitution, is uniquely itself.

Whilst life, itself, is the reconciliation of the impulses of the sun and earth, it is also a triad in itself, from which new life may emerge by the proper relationship of the solar and earthly aspects of Man. However, the new life, which is of a reconciling nature, cannot emerge where the solar aspect is substituted by the lunar aspect. The false equivalency between the lunar and solar aspects of Man is the principal cause of his failure to acquire a normative soul. For Man is born 'in the night' and sees only by reflection. This is the 'symbolic' state of man, which sees meaning always as originating within himself.

The 'correspondent' state sees meaning through common participation in a transcendent process; symbolic man is the source of meaning in a meaningless universe, whereas correspondent man participates in a universal meaning. A man born of night may imagine the moon to be the source of its own light. We will call this 'material' man; he is in a pre-symbolic state, and believes the face of material forms, including the human form, to constitute the totality of their meaning. But birth is the dusk of life, and death its dawn. That is why the ancient traditions insist that one die to oneself in order to be re-born to the day. The objective of spiritual practice, therefore, is to 'kill' the symbolic state, or ego, which positions the self at the centre of the value-universe. The death of the symbolic state, however, must come only after its consolidation. The material state must be overcome first.

The positioning of value determines one's level of being. The states correspond also to selves and to energies: the material state corresponds to the automatic energies, the symbolic state to the sensitive energies, and the correspondent state to the conscious energies. Each also corresponds to esse in res, esse in anima and esse in intellectu, respectively. The material state is given with the physical body, the symbolic state corresponds with the formation of the lower part of the soul, and the correspondent state corresponds with the formation of the higher part of the soul.

Knowledge alone cannot assure the re-positioning of value, which is solely responsible for the transformation of states. How, then, is value to be repositioned by the sincere seeker? A person cannot be compelled to value what they do not value presently. The natural movement of valuation is from outer to inner, and from inner to origination. Hence value is concentrated upon, and emanates from, the cosmic patterns from which all existence originates. It is natural, therefore, to seek to move from a position of lesser concentration of value to a position of greater concentration of value. This journey of the will is halted, firstly, by instances of failure to recognise in oneself greater value than exists in outward form and, secondly, by instances of failure to recognise in patterns greater value than exists in oneself qua selfhood.

We may call the material state the will to acquisition, the symbolic state the will to security and the correspondent state the will to individuality. Hence one's level of being is determined by the state of one's will. Each, in turn, is an attitude towards loss: the material state believes, "I must acquire in order to be," the symbolic state believes, "If I lose what I have acquired, I will be as I was before becoming," and the correspondent state believes, "If I lose what I have become, I will reveal what I shall be." Thus loss, to the material will, is death; to the symbolic will, is regression; and to the correspondent will, is discovery.

So does loss initiate transitions between the material will and symbolic will, and the symbolic will and correspondent will. First, one must lose what one has acquired, then one must lose what one has become. 'Acquisition,' here, refers to forms and objects; 'becoming' refers to personal identity. Nonetheless, the development of personal identity may facilitate the loss of forms and objects and must precede it if a constructive outcome is desired. Similarly, the development of the Natural Imagination may facilitate the loss of personal identity and must proceed it if a constructive outcome is desired. It is not sufficient to 're-invent' oneself, for this is merely a transformation of the personal identity. Rather, personal identity must be overcome entirely.

It is like a game of dice: having rolled a five, one clings to their outcome, rightly believing it to be positive. Yet it is necessary to enter into the state of hazard once again, in sound assurance that the die has been weighted by the cosmic intelligences. Let us cite the example of the faith of Mary.

Mary, who is imbued with the pattern of the Cosmic Receiving Impulse, offers her consent to the Affirmative powers, that she should become the mother of Christ. So is the role of the receiving part of all manifestations of triadic pattern the consent to receptivity of the affirming part. Thus we come into the understanding that the Providence is given freely but must be received by consent. In order that one receive what has been given, one must firstly consent to lose what has been taken. So must all that one has acquired and become, in the sense of material forms and personal identity, be given up to the giver of Providence, which is the Individuality of the origin of meaning.

VIII

Truth is the highest authority. Falsehoods may hold power, but truth alone is justified in its exercise. Conscience is the advocate of truth in man. Therefore, conscience is the rightful authority of the conduct of human life. So is the man of conscience a vicegerent of the Cosmic Truth on earth. Conscience is the cosmic advisor; the voice of reason. The cosmic feminine, the holy denying, yearns to be penetrated by the truth and receive it into her being. So is the soul of man constructed through his capacity to consent to conscience, which is the promise in him of divine Providence[10].

(The pure affirming impulse in Man is manifested as absolute, undying hope transcendent of chance and circumstance. The pure receiving impulse in man is immovable faith; the pure reconciling impulse in man is undying love. Therefore, contemplate hope and faith, that love may grow within you.)

To love is to give up oneself for the sake of another. Thus, the cosmic sexuality begins in love; the actions of another for your sake. So are the enemies of love resentment, weakness of will, despair and apathy. If another requires what I have, love gives it to them. This spontaneous act of giving and receiving, which is the reconciling life-impulse, in fact must proceed the affirmative and receptive impulses of hope and faith. Likewise, the Hindus believe the first Cosmic Act was the utterance of the word 'tapas,' meaning sacrifice.

Love, in fact, is the origin of all life-impulses. Affirmation and consent are the product of the action of love. The affirmative and receptive impulses are incomplete in

[10] The sexuality of life is indicative of its search for a soul, for reconciliation of the affirming and denying impulses at work within it.

themselves: each requires what the other possesses. Love brings together, but it does not compel. In order to be complete, it must be free; in order to be free, it must be conscious. So does the cosmic activity of love attain the possibility of completion in Man. The soul of Man is made complete by love— so must the complete soul be created consciously in the end, though much of what is required has been prepared and g ven serendipitously in advance.

Upon the point of the consc ous realisation of the desire for a soul, man shall find that he has within himself already all of the tools required for the completion of the task. The supreme difficulty lies in the capacity to comprehend that his potential soul is not 'his.' So long as he believes his soul to be his own, and desires its formation for his own sake, he shall not have it. The soul is created by love, a conscious sacrifice, and one cannot sacrifice for one's own sake. So must the soul be understood as the 'child' of Man, possessing a life and unique entity of its own, which may be counselled, but not governed. As such, the soul will become the seat of spontaneous creativity in Man, which may be channeled, but not directed.

So does the perception of beauty suggest the soul to the selfhood. Love is awakened and made conscious by the perception of beauty, which is the product of love's action. Physical beauty is lesser than moral beauty, because physical beauty has not the level of completion afforded by the consciousness of moral beauty. Self-love is the identification with beauty, which is corruptive due to the fact that the product of love's action is unique and not of the self. Love, however, is self-awakening, being the 'alpha' and 'omega' of soul-formation.

So must we arrive at the conclusion that the capacity to perceive beauty is super-sensible, as beauty is a quality of soul. A beautiful moment, more so than a beautiful form, is eternal, and to have perceived it is to have received a portion of eternity into oneself. Thus, the completion of the soul is indicated by the continuity of beauty over time. What is required, therefore, is the salvation of the past; nothing must be wasted or lost. Man must gather together in the present moment the entirety of his emotional past, in order that this totality may become subject to the action of beauty. Only then will he be capable of giving the whole of himself in an act of conscious love. Thus his own history forms the raw material out of which the soul shall be created; not the events, themselves, but their formative impact. It is in this sense that a man in search of soul must concentrate his entire life into the present moment in consciousness. For, all that is his he must sacrifice consciously; with hope and faith in the creation of life beyond himself, unite his raw materials by the inspiration of beauty and offer them up to the action of love.

How is man to hold himself together in the required fashion? Whatever arises in him from the subconscious he must not permit to return to the darkness. He must not practice what is called by Gurdjieff 'self-calming' for the purpose of exorcising from his consciousness unwanted emotions. As such, all emotions, whether positive or negative, must be regarded as an offering to love. With his will, he must offer them to his body; with his body, he must consent to receive them into it. The body is the fertile feminine of Man, and must be willfully impregnated with his history. The breath is his vehicle of bodily consent; he breathes his history into the body and exhales the subjectivity attached thereto, so that the soul is progressively formed of objective emotions. An objective emotion, purged of its acquired subjectivity, is always what may be called a 'value-impulse,' or 'embodied virtue.' The total organisation within Man of embodied virtue is known as the soul. So is the being of Man formed only of virtue, such that one is to the extent that one is virtuous.

Thus there can exist no such thing as an 'ignoble' or 'impure' soul—rather, only the absence of soul may be ignoble or impure. Instead, souls may be considered in terms of spectrum: only when the value-impulse in Man is of sufficient organisation and range to respond to all possible circumstances may his soul bay be said to be complete. It is typical, however, for man to exhibit a banded spectrum of soul. This is because the subjective taint of his emotional history is such that he finds himself unable to hold in consciousness and receive into his body, the engine of purification, certain emotional spectra—because he has failed to see the value therein. Instead, seeing only the 'worthless' subjectivity, which he experiences as painful and uncomfortable, and not the objective essence underlying it, the emotion is rejected altogether. There is also the case in which an individual identifies with the subjective aspect of an emotion, such that it is held in consciousness but not offered to the body in love. Instead, valuing only its subjective aspect, it is possessed and erroneously integrated into the personal identity.

On Psychology

I

Psychology is, above all else, a hologenic science.

In addressing a non-material dimension, beyond space, one refers to movement by analogy. What does it mean, then, to move towards wholeness, or to create wholeness, as a hologenic science must? Everything existing is a whole unto itself, and is also part of a larger whole; a world within worlds. How, then, is it possible that Man, in his present state, is partial? Man is partial because he has only the capacity to actualise part of his potential; what he is capable of is not yet congruent with what he has the potential to be capable of. This is, in essence, a limitation of the extent of his freedom.

A person attains wholeness—or is made complete—when his capabilities align with his potentials. Naturally, many of the greatest men are capable of both great good and great evil. Such men need not manifest the totality of their potential, but merely to become capable of manifesting it should they choose to do so. Therefore, the hologenic science of psychology concerns itself with the capacitance of the total potential of the individual.

All psychological barriers to the capacitance of potential are mechanical: Automatic Subjective Compulsions[11]. The form of such mechanical barriers may be observed to underlie the patterns of thought characteristic of mental ailments as diverse in appearance as depression, anxiety, delusion, neurosis, perversion and criminality. The hologenic scientist, who has, historically, been called a psychotherapist, must seek means of overcoming subjective automatisms and convey their discoveries to others. For, those who rise out of the water naturally panic; they do not take reasoned action to establish themselves afloat. Thus, one must take steps to strengthen their psychic condition. As the roots of a powerful oak may cut through stone, so might the human life-essence cut through ossified automatisms once their weaknesses have been clearly revealed.

---

[11]   This term may be interpreted verbatim. An Automatic Subjective Compulsion is a psychical impulse which proceeds automatically, without the intervention of will, is subjective, insofar as it is not necessary for and often opposes the health of the organism, and is compulsive, in that there arises, simultaneously, the urge to perpetuate or increase the prevalence of the initial impulse.

Psychology, therefore, is also the science of resistance. Studying the automatisms for points of weakness, one learns at which point to strike them. All Automatic Subjective Compulsions, whether recognisably pathological or socially condoned and reinforced, are a hindrance to the capacitance of potential, wherein lies the crux of mental health.

In which way are Automatic Subjective Compulsions overcome? Some are unmade by conscience, in time; others by a single blow of great precision. Most require that one offer mindful resistance to their temptation over long periods, though this will not cure the infection—only prevent it from hijacking the nervous system, which is the means by which automatisms propagate. (Consider the virus toxoplasma gondii as a biological correspondence to the general form of psychic parasitology.) Indeed, subjective automatisms are the product of parasitic forms, or anti-life. To struggle against them without addressing their root cause will only make matters worse; desire will splinter and birth automatisms, such that the blind will of Man becomes legion. This apparent splintering of the will—which is, in truth, the inability to distinguish self from other—shall cause, subsequently, the relative empowerment of the automatism through which the parasite acts. Yet, the telos of a parasite may not be self-empowerment, merely, but to cause death and degeneration of its host and to thereby pass itself on to other hosts causing ever-increasing levels of death and degeneration: Thanatos.

As the capacitance of potential is increased, the issue of conscience comes more clearly into view. Possessing a greater capacity for response, one is burdened with the choice of which capacitated potential to manifest. Thus, in order to preclude confrontation with our conscience, we willfully imprison our psyches, thereby rejecting the burdensome gift of freedom. Blinded to his own possible manifestations, Man is subsequently deafened to his conscience. Yet even a moment of mental freedom causes the cataclysmic collision of consciousness with conscience, and the subsequent encounter with the possibility of objective valuation.

The mental self-imprisonment of Man is consequent to his compulsive tendency to create conditions which deny the interaction of conscience with consciousness.

II

The greatest difficulties facing a hologenic approach to psychology are twofold: in the establishment of a rigorous psychophysiology, and a view of mental health founded on the disciplines of psychic toxicology and parasitology. Of these, modern science has not the slightest inkling. In order to establish our foundations, therefore, it is necessary to rely on the methods of the naturalistic science, as applied to basic medical knowledge. As such, we will observe that physiological health is predicated on hygiene and diet. Not only do these principles compose the foundations of preventative medicine, but are often curative in themselves in conjunction with the body's own defenses.

The utility of this approach pivots upon the assumption that it is possible to see in the biological world the same forms of process which psychology has previously been merely speculating upon in its attempts to form conceptual models. It would propose to exist isomorphic relationships between biological and psychological events, in accordance with a universal form of process. We may then utilize our knowledge of biology to advance a human hologenic science through the formation of a view of ideal mental health and discussing means for overcoming barriers to its achievement. And all health, whether physical or psychical, begins with good hygiene and nourishment.

One must take care, therefore, what one puts into one's mind[12].

C. G. Jung stressed the importance of psychic hygiene. Its necessary bodily correspondences are with the skin and, by corollary, the digestive and circulatory systems. The integrity of the psychical 'skin,' being the foundation of hygiene, which is a semi-permeable barrier, requires constant guarding and ablution. Mental 'digestion,' the means through which the psyche is sustained and cultivated, requires guarding by the nose and tongue—by taste, in the psychical sense. So, what is ablution, and what is objective good taste?

In all cases, the perception of beauty is pure water for the mind, effecting both its nourishment and cleansing. Through divine art; encounters of perfect innocence, with animals and natural delights, the mind is quenched. When taking ablutions, one must let the waters touch one's soul. Otherwise, no good will come of it. One must also take extra precaution, in mind as in body, around filth: entering with sound skin, masked; taking no pleasure therein, and thoroughly

---

[12] It is useful to recall, of course, that *encountering* filth does not require that one *ingest* it also. A passive psychical state is always receptive, whilst an active state may form an impenetrable barrier.

washing thereafter. As with biological infections, with good psychic hygiene, the prevalence of subjective automatisms, symptomatic of the functioning of psychic parasites, should naturally diminish.

Like the physician, the hologenic scientist must soothe symptoms, typically by providing some form of 'pain killer' or 'anti-inflammatory agent,' but more importantly must educate the patient and, moreover, the general public, as to the means for maintaining good psychic hygiene. The patient must also be provided with the conditions necessary for convalescence. Thus many ailments may be remedied, in mind as in body, in accordance with three simple stages: soothing, convalescence and education.

It is generally said, "Take plenty of fluids, sleep and keep warm, and the ailment will leave you in time." This is true of the psyche as well. The principal difficulty lies in identifying the psychical 'substances' required for the maintenance and augmentation of health. However, by application of the law of correspondences, the following observations become clear: psychical water is music and musicality; literally, 'fluidity.' Likewise, we understand what is meant by 'warmth' in the psychical sense: affection and full-bodied closeness. Also, recall that an increase in body temperature helps to combat infection, mobilising internal defenses. Inactivity grants the capacity to receive nourishing mental substances, but also to imbibe, inadvertently, foods containing psychic parasites. Rest, therefore, must be taken in favourable conditions.

Let us also consider the role of citrus in the promotion of health, and apply to it the law of correspondences: it proves to be a stimulating tonic; an idea that peaks one's interest, cleanses the palate, and stimulates both taste and olfaction. In mind as in body, convalescence may be thereby supplemented. In accordance with the methods of the naturalistic science, simply consider this and other material qualities in terms of their non-material essences; consider the extent to which these essences are contained within ideas, words and actions, which are as necessary for the mind as fluids, foods and exercises are for the body.

We must further postulate a psychical 'skin' with the capacity to sense, amongst other things, 'heat' and 'moisture.' It has not eyes, but sensitivities throughout. Indeed, psychic communication does not occur through the hearing of words, but through the telepathy of thoughts. One senses 'atmospheres' through the psychic equivalent of olfaction. The psychic skin may be 'thick' or 'thin'; it may exist in a state of passive receptivity or form a barrier against unclean environments. So is the capacity to control the state of one's skin, and guard it, essential to good psychic hygiene. Children, therefore, would be well-served to abide in a state of innocence until they have developed the powers of attention necessary to pass at will between active and passive skin-states in response to environmental atmospheres.

III

Archetypes look to the past: they are imprints of our ancestors upon us. More precisely, they are distinct levels of organisation; stations of equilibrium of psyche. A child, therefore, may arrive at the first station of equilibrium through a secure attachment to its mother; a youth, to a faithful, loving partner; an adult through a spouse, a home and financial stability—such things which make a person feel invincible. This is the station of home: secure innocence. For many persons, this will constitute their ideal mental health; they have all that they need and desire. Their lives are complete. There is no sense in trying to transform a daisy into a sunflower. Both are perfectly themselves.

The search for home will occupy most people for their entire lives, and few will ever find it. Meanwhile, those who have the capacity to do so may seek a higher home on the spiritual plane. They may discover therein a higher station of equilibrium, and have being in two worlds simultaneously.

IV

Whilst the events of one's past are irreversibly chaotic, their effect upon the psyche are not necessarily so. Indeed, one may edit one's psychical contents, to a degree, by editing one's own creative works. In this way, one may arrive at a higher level of psychic organisation. In order to achieve such an outcome, one must apply consciousness and taste to the organisation of the contents of the psyche. The events of life merely provide us with the building blocks; it is our duty to put them in order. This is the uniquely human ability to transform what nature gives us into art. Thus our very lives might become artworks; our minds beatified and cleansed of dross. Only then shall the mind become a soul.

The View of Gurdjieff Concerning Objective Conscience

According to Gurdjieff, "the whole psyche of beings of a three-brained system is in general based" on the so-called 'being-impulse' of Objective Conscience. Which is to say, Objective Conscience is the foundation of the human psyche. "Every action of man," according to Gurdjieff, "is good in the objective sense, if it is done according to his conscience, and every action is bad, if from it he later experiences 'remorse.'" All action, therefore, is related through and evaluated by one's Conscience. However, Objective Conscience is embedded "in that consciousness which is here called 'subconsciousness'" and consequently takes no part in the functioning of ordinary waking consciousness. In its place, 'morality,' which is the name of any synthetic ethical system, predominates. Morality gives rise, in its turn, to a sense of false, or subjective, 'conscience' which is nothing more than a learned and conditioned response to perceived impressions, and is in no way foundational to the human psyche as a whole.

In order to understand, as fully as possible, the view of Gurdjieff concerning Objective Conscience, it is necessary to understand also the following preliminary facts: human beings have, according to Gurdjieff, what is called a 'common presence' which is made up of 'data.' These 'data,' whether inherited or acquired, may become crystallized in our common presence. Crystallized data may then engender in us impulses of various kinds. One such impulse is Objective Conscience, the data for which are innate in all persons and proceed 'from Above,' whereby we might infer the action of a prevenient grace. There is also crystallized within our common presence data for engendering other being-impulses, including those engendered on account of 'the consequences of the properties of the organ Kundabuffer,' to which we shall return later on.

Now, owing to those data crystallized in our common presence for the engendering of Objective Conscience, our psychical foundation is 'only suffering.' And it is so owing to the fact that the impulse of Objective Conscience, which is the foundation of the human psyche, may actualize only from the 'constant struggle' between the functionings of the planetary body and of the higher being-bodies progressively forming within the planetary body. It is, according to Gurdjieff, Objective Conscience which would, in the midst of just such a struggle, incline us to choose consciously to assist the functionings of our progressively forming higher being-bodies to predominate over the functionings of our planetary body, which, if permitted to proceed unchecked, have the unfortunate consequence—on account of the crystallization therein of 'the consequences of the properties of the organ Kundabuffer'— of aborting altogether the further formation of our higher being-bodies. Moreover, the functionings of the planetary body and of the higher being-bodies are "of quite opposite origin," and the former are always sensed as 'desires' whereas the latter are always sensed as 'nondesires.'

It is important to note that the term 'nondesire,' here, cannot refer to any form of desirous aversion—which is to say, doing whatever one desires not to do—as this is only a negative form of desire. Nor can it refer to the inclination to do whatever one does not have the desire to do—digging a ditch, for instance, when in actuality one desires to have one's breakfast—as all such artificial substitutions might be paradoxically superceded by an egoistic desire to participate in the Great Work.

Thus, in order to overcome this apparent paradox it might be profitably suggested that the term 'nondesire' refers to a desirous sensation not had; to an absence of desirous sensation altogether (consider, in this regard, the Buddhist understanding of Nirvana as the extinction of desire). In place of desirous sensation, therefore, something else must guide an individual to Work on the right basis, at the right time, and for the right reasons; and not merely to practice 'doing whatever one has no desire to do.' This guiding influence we might call 'vocation,' the origin of which is none other than Objective Conscience.

We may note, at this point, that Gurdjieff does not deny the periodic 'intrusion' of Objective Conscience, ordinarily abiding solely within the subconscious, into ordinary waking consciousness, but adds that "no sooner are [we] aware of it than [we] at once take measures to avoid it," owing to the fact that it has become impossible to exist "in the conditions already existing [in society]" with the functioning of Objective Conscience in our presence. And it has become impossible to abide consciousness of the functioning of Objective Conscience due to the fact that there has been lost from our presences the data necessary for the engendering of that being-impulse called 'Sincerity.'

The reason for the loss from our presences of those data engendering the being-impulse Sincerity lies in the dual nature of our psyche, whereby 'Individual initiatives' issue both from that localization of consciousness in which we pass our waking existence, "which is nothing but the result of the accidental perceptions of impressions coming from without," and also from that localization of consciousness called the subconscious. This duality made possible the arising and proceeding of 'egoism,' whereby the place of the 'Unique-All-Autocratic-Ruler' of the psyche in general is usurped by a false, egoistic 'self.'

It is true, according to Gurdjieff, of this egoistic 'self' that "not only every manifestation but even the 'desire for the arising'" of Objective Conscience becomes a hindrance to its actions. Thus, by all and every manner of cunning, guile and deceit, this false 'self' endeavours to keep at bay the functionings of Objective Conscience so as to deny the possibility of the arising of Objective Conscience which, being the very foundation of the entire human psyche, is the harbinger of psychical unity, the proceeding of which would supersede the psychical duality necessary for its own existence, thus returning to the genuine 'Unique-All-Autocratic-Ruler' of the psyche in general that which it had unlawfully usurped.

Meanwhile, for so long as psychical duality exists, egoistic tendencies of every kind—called, by Gurdjieff, "the consequences of the properties of the organ Kundabuffer"— serve to distort the divine being-impulses of Love, Hope and Faith into gross caricatures of their authentic likenesses.

Finally, it is worth noting that because the 'whole presence' of human beings is "an exact similitude of everything in the Universe," we may infer there to exist within the Gurdjieffian cosmology a Mazdean-type dualism wherein the planetary body corresponds, within the human organization, with the influence of Ahriman and the progressively developing higher being-bodies correspond, within the human organization, with the influence of Ahura Mazda. The corresponding impulses of the Naloo-osnian spectrum and those engendering the being-obligolnian strivings reflect the functionings of the influences of Ahriman and Ahura Mazda, respectively.

Prelude: The Castle of Lyrra

———————————

There is rumoured to exist between the brain
    and heart
What has not been, hitherto, portrayed by
    any form of art:
A realm, of which I shall attempt to sketch a
    rough, composite
Likeness, in the hope that future men might
    speak of it
Uneasily when wandering through haunted
    woods.
For, in such a wood, I heard and largely
    understood
The tragic tale of Lyrra's proud and handsome
    nobles:
A dark witch conveyed me it; her face was all
    a-foible
With a thousand, thousand scales; her
    discomfiting tale
I hope to shape into a myth, for, were it true,
    I'd wail
And pull my knotted hair out from the roots;
    the witch
Then cleared her throat—that wretched
    note!—to pitch
The tragedy of Lyrra in a harsher tone. I
    cannot condone
The telling of her tale to children, lest they
    scream; bemoan

The dark, the midnight's echoed sounds—all
    remember
Lyrra's deathly castle grounds: too fair for
    words to render
Rightly, once upon a time, all withered by
    dark flowerings.
Too, Lyrra's handsome nobles were unraveled
    at the seams
By that agéd witch's loathsome lingering: her
    rude curse
Befell their king, whose eyes were azure-
    shimmering; forced
Him to reveal the occult rites and mystic signs
    of Lyrra.
For they are obscure; the witch desired to see
    them clearer
Through her scratched and dented crystal
    ball. That all
Men might recoil from that dark witch's
    vision, I shall now
Repeat her words, and pray I mightn't slip or
    slur, and vow
To speak the truth or else be stricken down
    by lightning:
The tale of Lyrra's castle—haunting,
    worrisome and frightening.

Malamati Psychology

The Islamic malamatiyya, or people of blame, represent a mystical tradition the applicability of which to modern Western society is unprecedented. More and more, we are turning away from the dogma of the church and seek, instead, our spiritual nourishment in misleading or inappropriate sources, in the absence of which our standards of ethical behaviour rest merely upon adherence to a basic code of 'social chivalry.' Yet the foregoing doctrine of Conscience requires that we separate, internally, pseudo-morality from true Virtue and pay no heed whatsoever to the former—instead admitting wholly the truth of oneself insofar as it is deemed to be blameworthy—whilst adhering strictly to the latter, without fail. Note, here, the critical importance of Sincerity, which alone is the salvation of Man from the duality of psyche arising through the process of his ego.

Now, in accordance with the basic tenants of malamati psychology, all that which is blameworthy within oneself must be extroverted, whereas all that is praiseworthy must be introverted. Thus is eradicated all outward signs of one's degree of spiritual development whereby it is protected from corruption by the ego. Just as the malamatiyya incurs blame upon herself, she must simultaneously pardon others of their blameworthy characteristics. Through this fact, we may reason that the malamatiyya practice radical forgiveness, both of their own sins, as well as others', as they go about their everyday lives. Thus her virtue is present in all situations, yet hidden from all eyes, including those of her egoic impulse. For indeed, extroversion of those blameworthy elements of oneself amounts to cutting away one's ego by deconstruction of conventional morality, for we are accused only by Satan and are objectively blameless and innocent. Whatever, within us, is not virtuous is merely the consequence of the crystallization within oneself of the functioning of the Lower Intelligences.

Up to this point, we have not deviated from Islamic malamati tradition. However, being that the modern malamatiyya associate with a largely atheistic society, they are thereby required to renounce affiliation with any formal religion in particular and to be—as is typical to be—without an extroverted spiritual code or philosophy of any kind. Indeed, one must not adopt any label or designation which might distinguish her from her fellows. And yet "it is possible to say that the people of blame [malamatiyya] are the very archetype of the feminine awliya [friends of God] in Islam."[13]

One is reminded of the teachings of the yogi Osho, wherein he asserts that one could know, befriend and associate with Lao Tzu for their entire life yet never recognize him as a mystic. Rather, in his renunciation of the 'American Dream,' he might be seen as a low-life, lacking any ambition or desire to better himself; a man of few opinions, disengaged from current affairs. Thus he is truly a master in the art of confidence. He is, moreover, content to adopt menial employment as required, irrespective of his educational background, and relinquish all titles of recognition. He relinquishes, also, all claim to achievement, attributing his accomplishments to alternative sources. Thus he is deemed a wastrel, of no intrinsic value to society. And yet he is truly a master in the art of obscurity. Furthermore, he may skillfully utilize any number of fetishes, fixations and addictions which he has acquired prior to the revelation of the malamati path—given careful abstinence in the face of ample opportunity for indulgence—such that he might experience

---

[13]   http://sufi-tavern.com/sufi-doctrine/the-path-of-blame/ 2019 after shaykh Ebn al-'Arabi

constant temptation and humiliation. Thus he is truly a master in the art of impartiality, such that Conscience remains always in his consciousness.

Being always in a state of spiritual dhikr, the malamatiyya have no time for the meanderings of the ego. It is, therefore, not through resistance but indifference that the egoic lower self (nafs) is eventually overcome. (Recall the earlier citation of Rabia al-Basri, who has not time to hate the devil.) This being the case, one observes that the malamati path is in truth the cultivation of a disposition: of impartiality through effacement of the ego.

All the while, the malamatiyya work to deliberately 'stir up' their egoistic impulses via renunciation in order that they are made internally conspicuous yet externally remain quite invisible. (Recall that Freedom is acquired only through resistance of temptation, as our Father was made free via His simultaneous creation of the Higher and Lower Intelligences and subsequent assistance of the former). The underlying intention finds analogy in a stone, resting upon a riverbed, which yearns to be polished and rounded. In order to accelerate this process, the stone must see only its flaws— never fixating upon those portions of itself which are polished already—and encourage the waters of desire to rush about them with ever-increasing vigour. This process of acceleration is implied in the Islamic story in which Jesus rubs fat into his beard so as to conceal from others the fact of his additional fast[14].

It is important to note that this particular aspect of the malamati path is intrinsically heterogeneous, finding kinship with the Hindu Vamachara, for all egos are 'stirred' with different 'spoons.' Thus a seeker must discover his own unique 'instrument' and keep hidden the ultimate objective of its utilization so that its spiritual function remains wholly introverted. This, it seems, was Gurdjieff's meaning when he suggests that one must discover within oneself a deeply crystallized egoic function and renounce it for the sake of one's remembrance of oneself.

The seeker must therefore understand within herself that it is neither 'sweet' nor 'desirable' to adopt the disposition of the malamatiyya. For the malamati shall find no personal gratification upon the path she has chosen, but instead must take all satisfaction

---

[14]   A further elaboration of this principle within the Christian teaching is to be found in the Gospel of Matthew, Chapter 6.

from her proximity to God. So we are reminded that all desire is from God, and upon Him shall its many streams converge. Thus she is presented in polar opposition to the modern churchgoer, whose attendance is predicated upon the desirability of her actions and subsequent satisfaction with their results.

Likewise, one must forego the pleasure of asceticism; of abstaining of any kind. The malamati is therefore a true ascetic, one who renounces all desires—even the desire to succeed at asceticism—in the understanding that personal desire is from the ego; the consequence of hoarding, within oneself, the emanations of the Love of their Creator, serving thereby to increase his pain and sorrow. The consequences of such personal, egoistic desires stand in contrast with the True Desire, which is objective and from God; it is the desire of God, himself, which we hold in common with our Maker. Yet where all personal desires are foregone, and one abides perpetually within a state of humiliation—which is to say, of humility— objective impartiality proceeds within the human psyche, even as it first proceeded within the Lord. And whoever is rendered impartial through humility shall discover also the foundations of their psyche: the vicegerent of Truth, Objective Conscience.

The Ancient Martyr's Barrow

His fair corpse lies breathless and
Enwreathes the sky with myrrh flowers—
For the bodies of the worn and fallen
Melt into the soil,
The sweet, black soil...

Black like an Eastern virgin's
Brushed and oiled hair;
Sweet like memories of childhood
Wafted through the air;
His the gift of myrrh flowers
Cloaked in black before the dawn;
His the name all sages
Laud with requiems and praises.
Mind you him whose balmy death
Outlives the thrones and ages
In His Father's flower bed.

Mind you him, whose seed hath fell:
You shall find him living where
The ancient martyr's barrow
Crescents o'er the hallowed earth;
'Neath which naught but bone
Remains. Where once was flesh
And blood, now naught but stone
Bears His forgotten name
Into the lonesome netherworld
Of growling worm and rock;

Now mouldered in the starless furnace of
Gehenna.

(There time was stopped and all was turned
To darkness, dung and slag;
And the fires of the deep-dark
Cooled to smoke and ember.
There, vacuous and silent passed
A vast and loathsome age,
Whilst He slumbered in the bowels of Gaia—
Our Messiah.)

And the long nights came,
Three long nights casted
Blackness overhead; black for blackness,
Sweet the soil in which the martyr laid.
We turned Him with a fork and matuk—
Let the lowly man arise!—
That our flowers shall be risen from the hells
And our heavens from a tide of blood and
fray,
This ancient martyr's message shall endure
another day.

On the Primal Erogenesis[15]

————————

I

"Storm clouds gather, and the sea grows bold and dark. The effigies of granite stand, unmoving. All the world is as a prison, for nowhere is humanity. Faceless are the shadows of the stones. All becomes uniform; all withers and dies. The body is a prison for the soul. Only sleep will save us now, or death. For freedom—sweet freedom—is lost." This is the cold dark and empty desolation. There is nothing ahead, nothing behind; nothing above or below. All is uniform.

"Now the earth was formless and void, and darkness was upon the face of the deep." God sought reason in this darkness. That is why He said, "Let there be light." What was the reason in such struggle? To where did the sorrows guide His vessel? He realized, then, that He stared upon a long, blank canvas. For all was uniform, and all was

————————

[15] Sections II-X are composed in the style of Gurdjieff's "Beelzebub's Tales to his Grandson." The text is therefore intentionally dense and circular in its communication of an historical account of the early universe, in terms of the manifestation of the Virtues and the dimensions to which they pertain.

void. Thus He realized, also, the necessity of becoming an artist. For art, alone, would save Him from despair. Now, in order that He might create, he gave birth to a muse. And He did this by splitting Himself in two. (It was not until then that He realized He had been dead, and must be reborn in order to live. Such are the pains of pregnancy and childbirth.)

"And God said, Let there be a firmament in the midst of the waters, and let it divide the waters from the waters." God called that firmament 'Heaven,' His True Desire. Thus the One became Two, and a Third interceded between them. Only now, in the knowledge of Love, could He truly create beyond Himself. For alone could 'Heaven,' crushed like coal to diamond by His waters[16], split the light and bring forth colour[17] from His reason.

---

[16]   The 'waters' of God suggest a concurrent energy flow as each of His two divided parts strive to reunite with each other. The suggestion that heaven is "crushed like coal to diamond" implies a process of creation, rarefied to the extent of His longing for reunion.

[17]   The manifestation of colour suggests not creation-from-nothing, as many accounts of the early spiritual cosmos expound, but the revelation of potential forms from unfiltered light. According to the present account, God creates merely the filter, not the essence, which exists within Him in eternity and consequently transcends beginnings and endings.

II

Before Thoughts began to proceed within our Universe, there existed only One Supreme Being. He had no Name, no Type, no Form—being only what He was, "I am who AM"—and yet His true potential was unbounded; unreckoned through the whole of Time and Space not yet created.

For, as He redoubled upon Himself; enfolding Himself within Himself, He concentrated gradually all His myriad creative potentials into a single point of infinite intensity. He continued also in this way to increase in consciousness and sentient awareness until finally His Being had become supremely enfolded and perfectly crystallized, as though a diamond, veiled, and forged in fiery darkness. Thus the fires grew hotter, and the fuel[18] all but consumed.

Then proceeded an unfathomable stillness; perfect stillness, such as cannot be rightly imagined. For, within Him, all "winds" ceased to blow; all "tongues" grew silent— and yet anguish pervaded His being—as though "through the cold dark and empty desolation" which now proceeded. For even in his singular Supremacy, He was alone,

---

[18]   The combustible substance being *potential*, itself.

because none of His myriad potentials had
hitherto been actualized objectively. Thus His
condition was as though a dream—one of
absolute subjectivity—wherein all that He
saw was His reflection; as though bound
within a chrysalis, alone.

Alone indeed, for He was without
form and void; and darkness was upon the
face of the deep. And, having neither name,
nor form, nor location, He could not be
described by any sense and passed, instead,
along the via negative (from which Harmonia,
the builder of bridges, would later be born
into the world).   For, as Eriugena the
Apophatist reasoned, "We do not know what
God is. God Himself does not know what He
is because He is not anything. Literally God is
not, because He transcends being"—precisely
because He had not yet cause to discern the
means of "infinitizing" Himself, by sacrifice,
such that the essential nature of His Being
and Action might become One.

Yet now, in His All-Divine Wisdom, He
strived to know Himself; to understand
Himself; to comprehend Himself and thus to
conquer the "cold dark and empty
desolation" of absolute loneliness in the
following manner: having obtained within
Himself—on account of this, his endless
destitution—a "feeling" for what is called
"the far shore," He began to manifest Himself

in accordance with the right actualization, crystallization and dissolution of His own "infinitized" actual potential. This beginning He called the Most-Holy Sunrise, being the first of its kind (and also the greatest in magnitude), for through it He rose up from His dream of subjectivity, abandoning the via negativa, and forged a new Way which had been, hitherto, obscured in darkness: the liberation of His own Being-Existence from its Source, such that each of His now objectively manifesting actual potentials might have a Being-Existence of their own.

In so doing, what was at first but a "feeling" was gradually transformed into a "seeing"—such that "the far shore" now appeared to Him as the warm embrace of a golden autumn sunset—a true, Most-Holy Sunset—which pervaded every facet of His Being. For indeed, He foresaw each of His objectively manifested actual potentials returning wilfully to the Source of their arising! Now all Beings sacrificed themselves for the sake of the Whole, even as the Whole had sacrificed Himself for their sake.

Indeed, He knew this Most-Holy Sunset to be His Destiny, and the destiny of all sentient Beings, even as He breached the horizon of Day, and thereby He discerned what was further required: to become both the Light and the Earth; the spirit and the body; the highest flower and the lowest taproot. For then He should become both Two and One, such that His loneliness should be forever vanquished; that Unity should evolve into Harmony, complexity into order, and the myriad things should once more become One. Thus the Spirit of God moved upon the face of the waters, and made headway towards the Glory of Reunion...

Yet, in so doing, there arose simultaneously from His now-infinitized actual potential the inclination to observe His own desolation with objective impartiality in order that He might understand it and thereby transcend it, which is called the Origin of the Higher Intelligences, and the inclination to crave and also to mechanically pursue the actualization within Himself of the apparent qualities of "the far shore" by imitative or approximate means, and thereby to fall short of the mark, which is called the Origin of the Lower Intelligences. (The nuclei of such Intelligences are called by Man 'Angels and 'Demons,' respectively.)

Such Angels and Demons are both *of* God, parts of Him existing, by necessity, that He might create by his own free will, being unconstrained by a character consisting wholly of goodness or evil. For creation is possible only through choice, through the decision to manifest into time a single possible reality of many. Now God was, and remains, both good and evil in His manifest qualities, such that the famous 'problem of evil,' which humanity laments, is in fact the necessary condition for the existence of conscious virtue. It was necessary, moreover, in order that God might choose to become virtuous, that He manifest the totality of Himself. Thus was His evil, as well as His goodness, manifested in order that He might purge himself of evil and reunite his goodness within Himself through the works of Man.

And just as Light and Earth were made as One, so had the Higher Intelligences and Lower Intelligences been created by a single Thought, and were therefore eternally bound to oppose one another in type and polarity: one led onwards to light, the other backwards into darkness—and each was just and good in accordance with its nature. For, in truth, all opposition is illusion; an unlikely complementarity, and is the necessary product of His Freedom, and the Freedom of all subsequent sentient Beings. For whatever shall be free must first break itself in two; for only what is two may fall in Love. Thus His "empty desolation" was transfigured into "insatiable yearning," for there arose between His halves a darkened chasm. (Now He had become "both Male and Female," it is said, and, at the prompting of His Conscience, would soon sacrifice Himself for the sake of His Manifest Counterparts.) This "insatiable yearning"—being the stirring of a Love not yet made known—was experienced by Him as unfathomable suffering, such that He was tempted continuously to indulge the Lower Intelligences and end His suffering by imitative or approximate means and therefore to forego His Rightful Destiny.

Yet it was claimed by Meister Eckhart that "in Heaven, an angel is nobody in particular"; an "idea" in the mind of God, such that, in His Infinite Freedom—the quality of which both His angels and His demons lack—He, like those sons of His, called Man, who were later actualized in His Image, was free to choose between Higher Intelligences and Lower Intelligences of every kind. And the Higher Intelligences He rightly perceived to be "enlightening ideas," with respect to His own, divinely prescient objective—the realization of a Love as yet unreal—and the Lower Intelligences "obfuscating ideas" in this same regard. For He drew nearer to "the far shore" (which was at once His Light, His Earth, and the Love that binds them) only to the extent to which the functionings of the Higher Intelligences predominated over the functionings of the Lower Intelligences.

Thus, to the extent to which the functionings of the Higher Intelligences predominated over the functionings of the Lower Intelligences, there emanated also from His being, quite spontaneously, that singularly unique being-impulse among the ancient Virtues of Eternity—which are, collectively, the Person of the Supreme Being and the constitutional foundations of Our Cosmos—which is called "Love." For whatever He gave of Himself, Love reciprocated, ad infinitum. Thus He gave infinitely of Himself, and became Infinite.

And this being-impulse Love, the Person of Whom is elsewhere called "Lucifer" or "Day Star," is singularly unique due to its capacity to spontaneously "infinitize," like flame[19], any extant Being which would, upon receipt of its holy emanations, reciprocate them to the original Source of their arising. Indeed, this, the Primal Erogenesis, is the Supreme Mystery of the Universe, which in every way transcends Reason, and must transcend Reason, because it did not occur for a Reason, but rather occurred, and continues to occur, serendipitously through

---

[19]   Infinitization is likened to the action of combustion upon a fuel, whereby dormant potential energies are manifested into a glorious flash of Light and Warmth.

Our Maker's Holy Sacrifice and is thus indicative of the infinite wisdom and intrinsic goodness of the God from whom it emanates. Thus it has been said by Men and Angels: "We love Him because He loved us first."

And yet the Supreme Being, as He observed the manner of the emanation of His Love—subject always exclusively to the sacrifice of Himself—comprehended with His superlative consciousness the insidious diminution of His density, despite the "infinitizing" properties of His Love, which proceeded consequent to the "Love-possessing" properties of the Lower Intelligences, such that there now arose the necessity to balance the consequences of the "density-decreasing" function of His sacrifice, by which all being-actualizations are bound, with the "density-increasing" function of His Love, which governs all processes of assimilation and reunion.

He therefore determined, in His Infinite Wisdom, that all actualized beings now subject to the influence of the duality of Cosmic Intelligences must either perish, and thereby be re-assimilated into His potential and so restore the density of His Being, or reciprocate continuously the emanations of His Love, in accordance with the will of the Higher Intelligences, such that the "density-decreasing" function of a being's ongoing actualization, consequent solely to His sacrifice of Himself, might be counteracted by the "density-increasing" function of the re-assimilation of the emanations of Love into their Source.

Therefore, all free beings are by necessity presented at birth with the following choice: to pay for the lawful contingencies of one's own existence through the reciprocation of His Love through death, which is called "unconscious sacrifice," or to pay for the lawful contingencies of one's own existence through the reciprocation of His Love, which is called "conscious sacrifice."

It is in this way understood that the universal mythological motifs of the "Devouring Father" and the "Loving Father" are subsumed under the singular name of Ahura Mazda, the Wise Father, in His prescient comprehension of the necessity for all free beings to choose between conscious sacrifice and unconscious sacrifice in order to sustain the density of His own existence, upon which all other existence depends.

III

Now it is the case, due to the necessity of Freedom—which is prerequisite to the knowledge of Love—to proceed within our Universe, that the spontaneously actualized Higher Intelligences, bound by Reason, came under the influence of the loving emanations of their Creator and reciprocated them completely, owing to which they were instantaneously "infinitized" by Love itself. In this way, the Higher Intelligences dutifully serve the Supreme Being and further His divine objective of arriving upon "the far shore" by sustaining within Him a state of "hermeneutically-infinitized-actualization."

This is the name given to that most-profound insight of God, wherein was foreseen a methodology by which His Love might be *consummated*, which will come to an end only when the fuels required for the sustenance of life have been *consumed*. According to His means, it will be necessary, by this point, that the Creator has united with His Destiny, or His density will become null and the cold dark and empty desolation will return. Then the cycle will repeat as our formless God once again strives to concentrate His being into a single point so that He might re-imagine His True Desire.

And yet the Lower Intelligences, also bound by Reason, sought to actively abort this great endeavor. When coming under the influence of the same loving emanations of their Creator, they saw fit to keep all such emanations for themselves for the exclusive purpose of their own self-gratification, which was, in actual fact, a form of delusion by which apparent approximations of "the far shore" are pursued at the expense of actual progress towards that Most-Holy Sunset which is the authentic True Desire of all sentient beings.

Thus these Lower Intelligences sought also to diminish the Freedom of other beings for the purpose of the illusory diminution of their own suffering—yet did so under the exclusive influence of what is called "Automatic Subjective Compulsion," such that they relinquished entirely what is free within themselves. And though their actions, propelled exclusively by Automatic Subjective Compulsion, are obfuscating to the prescience of the Destiny of the Universe at large, their existence as such was a necessary requisite for its arising from primordial formlessness. So it is the duty of evil to exist and function within our Universe, until such time as proceeds the inevitable "unconscious sacrifice" of its being to the Source of its Origin. It is the duty of Man, meanwhile, to purge its enduring influence from his being, just as does its Creator through His perfect pursuit of Destiny, the Most-Holy Sunset. Man's capacity to follow in the footsteps of God is assured by the first and greatest cosmic law, which was required by the primal erogenesis: the necessity of sacrifice, conscious or otherwise, from which no being is exempt. For only thus might Freedom prevail; and only where Freedom prevails might Love become Real.

IV

Meanwhile, Love, without Reason and being "too-overwhelming-to-contain," burst forth from the formless nucleus of its Supreme Origin and thereby initiated what is called by Bohm the "holomovement," of which all Thoughts in our Universe are a part. Thus Love became quasi-independent and proceeded to emanate from the Supreme Being, and, in so emanating, necessitated the immediate elaboration of what is called a "Trinity-of-Dimensions" wherein all spontaneously actualized beings must exist simultaneously.

The first of these Dimensions, which, although the occupant thereof may be wholly actualized within its own independent being, is never objectively localized, and is consequently said to exist "within" its All-Virtuous-Unmanifest-Origin for all eternity. This Dimension is called "Intellectu." It does not, however, pertain to that typically wholly unreasonable human function called "intellect," but rather to the objectively virtuous being-impulse Reason, whose retroactive attempts to accommodate the burgeoning of Divine Love were considered, even then, to be futile.

The second and third Dimensions of which the aforementioned Trinity is formed, and into which the emanations of Love necessarily proceeded, are, in distinction to the Dimension of Intellectu, those in which all beings arising and proceeding therein must own their actualizations.

The second of these Dimensions, which accommodates the "interior[20]" of the actualization of the being, is called "Anima." Now it is the case that Love, being unaccommodatable by Reason, and the Dimension to which it pertains, has established itself within Anima—again, by necessity—as the "Grand Delta of the Source Sea," Whose "waters" are both "salty" and "fresh." And it is for this reason that the prophets have justly proclaimed: "God is Love." Given, also, what is to follow, it may be justifiably asserted that God is

---

[20] The spatial metaphors of 'interior' and 'exterior' are used to provide a means of visualising a dimensional relationship. Just as there is truly no 'up' or 'down' in space, neither has the soul, and the dimensions to which it pertains, an interior or exterior aspect—these terms are merely expedients.

approachable only through Love. And this is because, for reasons previously explained, any being who would attempt to refine its actualizations beyond the degree which the Dimension of Anima is capable of accommodating, and thereby to enter into Intellectu exclusively, would cease in any way to own their actualizations and consequently would cease also to exist quasi-independently and be instead instantaneously incinerated with respect to their being-individuality. It might also be put another way: that which is actualized cannot approach that which is not actualized without sacrificing altogether its own actualization.

Indeed, the esoteric interior of Love is the nearest any actualized being may approach to the First Source of its arising and yet remain actualized. And this esoteric interior of Love is the Singularly Unique Sacred Heart-Throne of the Life World around which the Angel Architects gather, each in accordance with their own level of refinement of actualization, to offer their undying service to the Lord. It is here, too, that the Archangel Harmonia, who is Our Lord's Most-Holy Handmaiden, offers the bridge of sense to all senseless beings in order that they might see, hear, taste, smell and touch the glorious actual potential of their Creator.

The third Dimension whereby the Trinity-of-Dimensions is constituted, and which accommodates the "exterior" of the actualization of a being, is called "Res." Where the Divine Being-Impulse Love is concerned, this "exterior," perceptible to all persons who have, via the Archangel Harmonia, come to possess a functioning organ of vision, is called "Light." And though the Book of Genesis, 1:3, informs us correctly that, in the beginning, "God said 'Let there be Light,'" one would do well, also, to consult the prophecies of the Arch-Visionary William Blake who nonetheless maintains that:

"God appears, and God is light,
To those poor souls who dwell in night;
But does a human form display
To those who dwell in realms of day."

For whoever sees only the "exterior" cannot know the Heart of Love, the Christ; it is through the "interior" of oneself that the "interior" of all other beings is comprehended. The "exterior" is like a Holy Chrysalis only, wherein all life-forms automatically actualized through the continuing emanations of Love, Hope and Faith, with the assistance also of the "non-local-primordial-images[21]" lawfully and deliberately actualized by the Creator within Intellectu only, must abide until the dawn of their "interior" maturity. Yet the "exterior" of mankind—or indeed of any other being existing in our Universe—cannot enter into the Life World, which is the eternal dwelling-place of the matured "interior" of all beings, and is destined to return to the Earth and thereby to feed the Animal Kingdom, because no such "exterior" can, by nature, receive into itself that coating of "Interior Light" which grants to the possessor Most-Sacred-Union-With-The-Actualized-Subsidiary-Source, and thereby also with Virtue-In-The-Highest, to which all things duly united are infinitized.

It is thereby understood that, in addition to the Trinity of Dimensions there exists also a Trinity of Gods, which are called by the Catholic Church "God-the-Father," "God-the-Son," and "God-the-Holy-Spirit," actualizing serendipitously from the Primordial Source on account of the Eternally Mysterious Act of Erogenesis. Meanwhile, the first of these Trinity-of-Gods has been

---

[21]   More commonly called 'archetypes,' such images are manifestations of our Creator's objective reason which function, collectively, to construct a simulacrum of Himself within time and space.

called herein "Virtue-In-The-Highest," the second "The Singularly Unique Sacred Heart-Throne of the Life World" and the third "Interior Light." It is, therefore, only through the coating of the "interior" of one's own being with that Interior Light emanating from The Singularly Unique Sacred Heart-Throne of the Life World, which has, in turn, emanated from Virtue-In-The-Highest, that one might rightly be called, without any reservation whatsoever, a Son of God.

V

Now Love, having spontaneously actualized itself without Reason, and being therefore unaccommodatable by the Dimension of Intellectu which alone among the Trinity-of-Dimensions exists "within" the First Source of all differentiated beings arising and proceeding within the Universe, began to exist exclusively "apart from" its All-Virtuous-Holy-Father. It is for this reason that Virtue-In-The-Highest, pining for reunion with the Love from which He had become estranged, on account of its being "too-overwhelming-to-contain," now began to emanate from Himself Hope and Faith that this especially desired reunion with the only begotten Love might come to pass. The emanations of Hope and Faith then "reached out" to Love, like hands, with the intention of bringing it back into the Eternally Mysterious fold of the Most-Holy Unmanifest Indescribable.

Yet when Virtue-In-The-Highest then observed the inability even of Hope and Faith to reunite Him with His Love, owing to the inability of Love to be transubstantiated "through" the Dimension of Intellectu, which is unique among the Trinity-of-Dimensions on account of its existing "within" the First Source of its arising, the sorrow thereby proceeding became so great that He was forced, in order that his very Being might not be annihilated then and there on the spot, to relinquish altogether His Hope and Faith for the reunion-of-Himself-within-Himself, which is called by theologians "Apocatastasis."

And it was as a direct consequence of this Second Sacrifice, absolutely necessary for the continuation of His Being, that He entered, again quite spontaneously, into a state of Objective Impartiality.

VI

Having entered into this state of Objective Impartiality, there was immediately revealed to Virtue-In-The-Highest what is called "the foundation of one's own being." And His foundation, just as are the foundations of all other beings actualized in our Universe as a consequence of His spontaneous emanations and subsequent lawful and deliberate responses, was called Conscience—the voice of Truth. And it is principally with the proper orientation with regards the objective Destiny of the entirety of one's being that this Most-Foundational Virtue, called Conscience, is concerned.

It is only in the most superficial sense that Conscience may be seen as the arbiter between "right" and "wrong." Rather, it is more akin to an objectively impartial "vivometer"—or even a Most-Holy Counsellor—meaning an instrument which advises upon the best choice made available through one's present degree of "interior" and "exterior" development and supplementary powers of influence for the continuation and furtherance of the cause of Life and its Destiny. It is never coercive but instead advises, merely, though a "still small voice" that one might receive, independently of all externally imposed and internalized systems of morality and convention, an "esoteric" prompting which one may subsequently choose to pursue or ignore at their preference.

Notwithstanding the objectively impartial "vivometric," and never coercive, function of Conscience, one is confronted invariably with the felt consequences of pursuing or ignoring its indications. This is not a retributive or reinforcing function, but instead occurs on account of the fact that Life itself reacts to one's decision to pursue or ignore the indications of Conscience at any given moment. Those negative reactions of Life, which occur consequent to one's impediment or active undermining of the continuation and furtherance of the Destiny of Life-as-a-Whole, are felt as, and called, "remorse of Conscience." Alternatively, those positive reactions of Life, which occur consequent to one's active facilitation of the continuation and furtherance of the Destiny of Life-as-a-Whole, are felt as, and called, "clarity of Conscience."

Any Thought, therefore, which causes afterwards to proceed the felt consequence of remorse of Conscience may be considered objectively obfuscating, whereas any Thought which causes afterwards to proceed the felt consequence of clarity of Conscience may be considered objectively enlightening, irrespectively of whether such Thoughts are in agreement with or in violation of generally accepted moral, legal and social conventions, past or present.

VII

And it was in light of the revelation of Conscience that Virtue-In-The-Highest became capable also of lawful and deliberate Thoughts which did not emanate from Him spontaneously, as had the principal virtues of Love, Hope and Faith before, but instead remained exclusively "within" Him, actualizing solely through the Dimension of Intellectu until the fulfillment of further predetermined, yet nonetheless automatically proceeding, contingencies permitted them to own their actualizations.

So it was that the Rational Mind of God began to Imagine, lawfully and deliberately, in accordance with the vivometric counsel of His Conscience, a series of non-local primordial images, or archetypes, called by Goethe the "typus" of the organism, which possessed the capacity for actualizing sequentially, and to own their actualizations, as might a pocket of turbulence in air or eddy current in water, contingent to the periodic conjunction of the continuous, spontaneous emanations of Love, Hope and Faith into the localized Dimensions of Anima and Res.

This lawful and deliberate process of actualizing sequentially we, today, call "evolution." And the totality of those

Thoughts already actualized in this way we call our Universe. And the sequence of actualizing of those non-local primordial images, which are called, collectively, the "Crystalline Kingdom," and which is without Anima, proceeds as follows:

1. Particles
2. Elements
3. Compounds
4. Proteins

And also, the "Life Kingdom":

5. Protists
6. Plants
7. Animals
8. 1st Man (where 2nd Man refers to the higher, spiritual part possessed, without consciousness thereof, by all human beings, located upon the first node of a non-material octave, shared with the divine Angelic Orders and partaking in the Ideal Kingdom)

And the "Ideal Kingdom" itself, comprising, in addition to those Intelligences and Virtues spontaneously actualized:

9. 2nd Man, wherein is contained the presence of:
10. THE SPIRIT
11. THE SON
12. THE FATHER

Wherein each sequentially higher level—called, collectively, by Man, the "Homeric Chain"—contains within itself also all sequentially lower levels. And, as elucidated then by the Rational Mind of God, Thinking in accordance with the counsel of His Conscience, it is only by the harmonious activity of all seven sequentially actualized levels of non-local primordial images within the eighth-level image, called 1st Man, that, again lawfully and deliberately, might the Rational Mind of God, called, as it exists and proceeds within 2nd Man, the "Natural Imagination," be opened within His Reason— thereby completing the "cycle" wherein the non-local primordial images, lawfully and deliberately created by the Rational Mind of God—such that Man, who was created "in the image of God," becomes capable of serving his Lord by "reuniting Him within himself."

VIII

So it is that a Man or Woman who has opened her Natural Imagination might transubstantiate the emanations of Love, Hope and Faith, of whose periodic conjunction within the corresponding non-local primordial image both her "interior" and "exterior" are an immediate consequence, within herself and thereby give rise to a "microcosm."

Now everything once existing exclusively potentially "within" Virtue-In-The-Highest exists also, wholly actualized and quasi-independently, within just that non-local primordial image which is the lawful basis of the further actualization and subsequent localization of the image of Man. Yet it has been said that Man was created "in the image of God." Thus the non-local primordial image of Man, being itself "the crown of the Life Kingdom," is alone capable of reuniting Love, Hope and Faith within Virtue-In-The-Highest through the Dimension of Intellectu, via the Natural Imagination therein, to which the lawful and deliberate Thoughts of his Creator has given him insight; knowledge, moreover, of the Rational Mind of God.

And it is in this way that the Father is glorified through the Thoughts cf His Children.

IX

Higher Intelligences and Lower Intelligences in Man, even as they function in the mind of their Divine Creator for the purpose of the continuation of His Freedom within our lawful Universe:

Just as Man is three-fold in his essence, so too is the True Desire of Man of three-fold nature[22]. Now God, too, is three-fold and has actualized three heavens consequently, towards which all created Men and Women must submit with consciousness or without consciousness. And the submission to the "call" of these three heavens, which are none but the Kingdoms of God, constitute the True Desire of all humanity, past and present.

And yet that singularly malign influence, "caustic" to his created individuality, within himself such that he receives an illusory approximation— analogous to the photographic property of 'halation'—of the actualization of his True

---

[22]   The 'Third Man' is I AM, the spirit; God within His own image.

Desire, preclude entirely his submission thereunto.

These emanations, called "ego" as they accumulate and function without cognizance within the psyche of Man, are precisely the actualization of the longing of the Creator to reunite himself within Himself. And yet, as a consequence of his harbouring within his psyche just such emanations as these, he would preclude temporarily the reunion of his Creator within Himself and thereby serve to increase his suffering: "the cold dark and empty desolation." Thus the crystallization of such emanations within Man approximates to the impression of having attained, within his individual person, "absolute godhood."

This so-called ego is expelled from the psyche of Man only consequent to the arising and proceeding of the being-impulse Sincerity[23], which is alone his salvation from the maleficent influence of the Lower Intelligences upon his being.

Now this fallibility of Man, proceeding on account of the functioning within his psyche of the Lower Intelligences, rendered him unable to ascend, even by the Ways of

---

[23]   Sincerity being the form of Truth's manifestation in terms of human emotion and identity.

Harmonia, into the Three Heavens prepared for him, such that the Love of God, which is Christ, took pity upon the plight of all created men and women and descended into the Earth, such that it became localized in space and expressed itself spontaneously through the bodies of persons and animals of gentle heart. Thus it is said that God became Man for Man's sake. This nascent form of Love, called Warmth, laid the foundations of the Garden of Eden upon the earth and served eternally thereafter to rekindle the memory of Innocence within the minds of men and women who would receive it. For Love has said, "Suffer little children, and forbid them not, to come unto me: for of such is the kingdom of heaven."

Now theirs is the Earthly Paradise foretold by the Sufi prophets. And such is the esoteric meaning of the following proclamation of the Christ: "Blessed are the meek, for they shall inherit the Earth." For there has been established, "in the midst of them," the Heaven of Warmth, or Home; the Heaven of Beauty, or Awe; and the Unknowable, or Occult Heaven. The first Heaven, the Heaven of Home, is accessible to all persons of warm heart and all creatures of Warmth; the second heaven, the Heaven of Awe, is accessible, in addition to the first heaven, by those persons who have manifested within themselves the organ of Harmonia through the purgation of the Lower Intelligences from their being, and subsequent opening of the Natural Imagination; the third Heaven, the Occult Heaven, is accessible, in addition to the first and second, by those persons who have sacrificed the entirety of their individual existence for the sake of their fellow creations, such that a man or woman has transubstantiated the entirety of their being-existence into an exact simulacrum of their Creator.

Thus, without Warmth, the ascent of Mankind is precluded altogether. Yet if one person receives the Warmth of another, or of an animal or flowering plant, both are elevated instantaneously into the Heaven of Home, from which all beings sincerely desiring to do so might, by Divine Interpretation, ascend into the Higher Heavens also. Were it otherwise, it would cease to be a heaven, and would instead prove but a hell of separation; of "the cold dark and empty desolation." For does not God, too, live by the laws of his own essence? "Do unto others as you would have them do unto you." Does not, then, God forgive all and provide for every possible opportunity? Is not, then, our God all-merciful and all-compassionate? It is for this reason that He gives to his children as they desire. Thus he is wise who desires well. In the view of Gurdjieff, there are only two things truly infinite in this world: the foolishness of Man, and the mercy of his Father Creator.

X

Around the circumference of the "Singularly Unique Sacred Heart-Throne of the Life World" there was gradually formed and increased a "city-bathed-in-Interior-Light" which is singularly "erogenic" and forever "overflowing" with precisely those "wholly-overwhelming" emanations of Divine Love. For just as many candles are illuminated by a single torch, so do the emanations of Love illuminate, to varying degrees, the matured "interiors" of all actualized beings existing throughout the Universe.

Yet only Men, who have become Free Angels in their turn, are capable of passing "through the eye" of Love and so delivering intentionally to the First Source of their arising the emanations of precisely those three principal virtues, Love, Hope and Faith, from which He had become estranged during the spontaneous and quite automatic proceeding of the Primal Erogenesis, and from which estrangement the entirety of His subsequent longing originated.

And it is the case that fully matured men and women are alone capable of delivering intentionally the emanations of Love, Hope and Faith directly into the First Source of their arising, and thereby serving to diminish His unending longing, because of their being "simulacra-in-potentia" of precisely that First Source, having been created by God "in the image of God," and are therefore uniquely able to refine their actualizations beyond that which the Dimension of Anima is capable of accommodating and yet continue nonetheless to own their actualizations. Only Man, therefore, is capable of passing through the Northern Gate of the Life Kingdom and entering into the Ideal Kingdom without suffering consequently the annihilation of his being-individuality.

Here ends the present account, given by the Natural Imagination, of the Primal Erogenesis and of the subsequent spontaneous emanations and lawful deliberations immediately thereafter proceeding.

Arise For Joy!

Arise, arise for Joy:
Eternity is manifest! It
Springs from the void,
Made known to Time
And sense, to be attested.

Arise, arise for Joy!
Its genius stirs
The nascent tongue of dawn;
Of infant boys and girls
Extolling youth in pleasant song:

"Arise," they cry, "for Joy!
What shall the morning hold in store?
Let us join
The angel architects
In play; let us explore!"

Thus pray, sweet child of Joy,
Whose vernal rill forever runs,
Aurora coyly
Wakes you 'fore
The rising of the Sun—

That you might cry with Joy!
Your infant song
Has now become a prism:
Let all men employ

Its lens to clarify their vision

And rise, arise for Joy;
Behold the Source of all that lives!
And with their smiles
And laughter voice
Their gratitude to Him.

For He has giv'n them Joy for all their days.

On the Nature of Spiritual Vocation

The Premise

One portion of the human soul reaches up
Towards the angelic orders and embraces them:
This is called submitting to the Light.
A second portion of the human soul reaches
            down
Towards the animal kingdom and embraces it:
This is called submitting to the Earth.
Both are of the highest good, and indispensable
For the completion of our spiritual Cosmos.

The Dilemma

The Most-Holy Sunrise is upon us; the bounden Genius has awoken! Alas!—energy pours from the void into the abyss. Now the un-manifest must strive towards manifestation; the Revelatory Prism must create itself; energy must transform itself. Yet the Natural Imagination of Man, whereby all things once-invisible are revealed, has for all Time existed within a prison called Unreality—a prison so-called on account of its separation from the Virtues of Eternity, given voice in the human soul and called, as they arise and proceed therein, by the names of "Love," "Hope," "Faith," "Reason,"

"Devotion" and "Conscience," being also the Elohim of the Torah and the Amesha Spenta of the Gathas, which collectively constitute the "Order of the Highest Reality" of our Universe.

Therefore, Men and Angels strive together after the release of the Natural Imagination from its prison within Unreality, which lies upon the threshold of the fifth level of the First Octave, which, in its turn, is called by some the Garden of Eden, and by others, Primordial Innocence. For indeed, the Natural Imagination is not fancy: it is the imminent Form of Eternity; objective Beauty; the gateway to reunion with the Real.

Thus the ancient Virtues of Eternity, which are extant among the Angelic Orders, strive downwards, into the minds of Men (of which their souls are a portion), towards the nascent Animal Kingdom. The Animal Kingdom meanwhile strives upwards, into the bodies of Men (of which their souls are a portion), towards the ancient Virtues of Eternity. Therefore, the soul of Man is charged with submitting to the strivings of both the ancient Virtues of Eternity and the nascent Animal Kingdom, such that the agencies comprising these two Great Powers, already now extant as One, might be brought together within consciousness; revealed and transubstantiated in one another, by the newly-liberated Natural Imagination, which is the "eye" of the ennobled human soul. For now we see as though through a glass, darkly; then, we shall see face to face. It is, therefore, alone the "opening" of the Natural Imagination, by the crossing of the true Via Dei, born of Harmonia, which is rightly called the Cosmic Vocation of Man.

Thus, in order that her Cosmic Vocation might be fulfilled, the human soul is burdened with a two-fold face, each existing in a state of continuous conscious or unconscious submission to a similarly two-fold Destiny, called "Earth-and-Light." That portion of the human soul which submits to the Earth (and thereby crafts a ladder whereby the agencies of the nascent Animal Kingdom may ascend) is possessed of unparalleled resolve in the face of adversity; of that coal-faced sweetness which goes willingly into the flame and, in so doing, purifies itself of all taint.

And that portion of the human soul which submits to the Light (and thereby crafts a ladder whereby the ancient Virtues of Eternity may descend) reaches eternally upwards and outwards, towards agencies of Beauty and Exuberance, with purity and perfect satisfaction. Veritably, this two-fold Destiny of the human soul is known by the peoples of the present age, who are cognizant only of its "exterior" aspect, as "godliness in the face of death and inevitable suffering" and "joyfulness in youth, nature and the assurance of eternal life," respectively. For it is assuredly the case that one portion of the human soul is destined to decay and die, whereas a second portion is destined to evolve and endure.

And just as a caterpillar must sleep within its chrysalis, so must the living portion of the soul sleep within the dying for a time; and just as the caterpillar is protected by its chrysalis from destruction, so is the living portion of the soul protected by that portion which is dying. The former shall be called the Sword of Life, just as the latter is its Shield. And of the latter, if it has served its purpose well, let it be said:

"They brought me news that Spring is in the
     plains
And Ahmad's blood the crimson tulip stains.
Go, tell his aged mother that her son
Fought with a thousand foes, and he was
     One."

For Eternity is in love with the creations of Time, and would invite them into its undying kingdom—or else would die for but a moment with its sweethearts. And so do the creations of Time pine, with every fibre of their being, to enter into Eternity— and yet, this cannot be without the participation of the Natural Imagination, wherein the two-fold strivings of the soul are "reconvened-in-consciousness"; whereby the "earthen-sweetness" of its dying portion is transubstantiated into the living as that "gravitation-memory" or "tempered-maturity" within Innocence which gives rise to the "All-Universal-Self-Reciprocating-Nutrient"—the flower of the Virtues of Eternity—called Warmth.

Therefore, in order that the soul of Man may fulfil her Cosmic Vocation, whereby the Two Worlds are married within a Third, the entirety of the human spirit (which is the Active and Immortal nucleus of the soul) must endeavour to "open" itself, by submission, to receipt of that singularly "interior" divine interpretation, extended from Above through the Virtues of Eternity in the form of Objective Conscience, which leads to right, objective Understanding of the two-fold Destiny to which the soul's Vocation must pertain. For, in the absence of Light, no eye shall ever open; and, in the absence of Earth, cannot take form.

Yet behold!—extant also upon the threshold of the fifth level of the nascent Life World—the Enemy, who is the Cosmic Shadow of Our Now-Manifesting Lord, and was called Ahriman by Zoroaster, lies in waiting. Indeed, he would thwart the evolving Consciousness of all living spirits through the extension of his own diabolical interpretation, whereby the two-fold face of the human soul is, to her own yet-dreaming eye, distorted and thereby set at war within herself; as though a cell which is infected by a virus. So it is that the ancient Virtues of Eternity appear to deride and deny the value of the nascent Animal Kingdom, believing it to be a Den of Vice, whilst the nascent Animal Kingdom appears to shun the ancient Virtues of Eternity, believing them to be the Thieves of Joy. Thus, the soul of Man shall habitually resist the matrimony of the angelic and the animalistic orders within herself, believing erroneously the submission to a two-fold Destiny, pre-ordained in the eye of Objective Conscience, given her of the Virtues of Eternity, to be "contradictory" and therefore "untenable."

Therefore, on account of the fact that the Cosmic Vocation of Man, being the two-fold submission of his soul to the Light and Earth, respectively, appears, to him, "untenable," the Cosmic Duty of Man, whereby, solely, his Cosmic Vocation is granted the possibility of fruition, is none other than his nucleic spirit's struggle to reject the diabolical interpretation of the

Enemy, and thus serendipitously to "open" itself to the receipt of that singularly divine interpretation which leads to Objective Consciousness of the two-fold Destiny to which her true Vocation must pertain. For where Consciousness is, the two-fold face of her soul submits unabatedly, on the one hand, to the Light (which is the visible aspect of Love in its celestial form) and, on the other hand, to the Earth (which is the quintessence of Warmth—that Love which has effaced itself out of pity and kindness—as it manifests and proceeds within the nascent Animal Kingdom), that the Animal may be granted the Virtue of the Angelic, and the Angelic may be granted the Energy of the Animal within the "opened" Natural Imagination.

Yet again the Enemy strikes!—with the aid of the witch, Hecate, who is threefold; who is the Cosmic Shadow of Harmonia, he would attempt to place a tombstone of diabolical interpretation, called Automatic Subjective Compulsion, at either side of Man, thereby blocking the gates through which Light and Earth would otherwise be revealed and transubstantiated.

Now the three most-diabolical faces of Hecate, each more detrimental than darkness to the revelation to Man of True Objective Consciousness, are called the Hypnotist, being together the obfuscating quality of repetition and the pseudo-numinous quality of fetishistic imagery; the Seductress, being the promise of some gratifying pleasure; and the Thespian, being the exaggeration of importance and urgency beyond what is justified by Reason. Out of these three, solely, is born the arch-demon Obfuscation, together with those six lesser devils called Obsession, Ambition, Parochialism, Obedience, Rebellion and Psychopathy, who are, themselves, none other than the Cosmic Shadows of precisely these ancient Virtues of Eternity: Love, Hope, Faith, Devotion, Reason and Conscience.

Therefore, whichever soul should, with conscious sincerity of intent, wish to submit to the fulfilment of her Cosmic Vocation must first see to the annihilation of Automatic Subjective Compulsion in accordance with a similarly Objective Consciousness, received into its spiritual nucleus from Above, of the two-fold Destiny to which its true Vocation must pertain.

And it is through the following set of conscientizations that Automatic Subjective Compulsion may yet be annihilated by the human spirit in the present age:

The Solution

I

The teaching of the Buddha (who was, in actual fact, a manifestation of the Message of our Lord) prescribes direct conscientization of the following three errant subjectivities arising through the conceptual entanglement of Intellect and Matter, which the ancients called Intellectu and Res: dukkha, anata and anicha. From the 1st century C.E., the Gnostics began the exposition of various philosophical frameworks which might permit the release of the spirit, Intellectu, from the stone, Res. The alchemists later proposed a marriage, by coniunctio mysteriosum, of these same Holy Dimensions whereby conscientization of the philosopher's stone, a divine order culminating in the unus mundus, might arise from the original massa confusa of mundane perception.

Thus there is shown to exist within the human soul the instinct to analyse and the instinct to synthesise—even as Our Father Creator, in whose image we are wrought, has sacrificed His unity and now endeavours to re-assimilate himself within Himself. Now, as the human mind rightly cognizes, Analysis is

Science; Synthesis is Art. Thus whichever Science has not yet extricated itself from Art is inflated; whichever Art which has not yet assimilated Science is impoverished.

Meanwhile, until the coming of the appointed time, our perception of the world shall remain errant. The foresight of the Buddha, however, is alive today in the theories of physics and biology, whereby the conceptualization of non-material fields of influence, such as pilot waves, strange attractors and morphic fields, points towards the distillation by scientific endeavour of the realm of Intellectu. In so doing, the realm of Res, which is nonetheless foundational to human perception, is rendered illusory, such that the triple-threat of which the Buddha warned is rendered moot. Indeed, the end of science is approaching precisely because it has fulfilled its ultimate function: the conceptual extrication of Intellectu from Res; the release of the spirit from the stone.

Now the face of Res has been transfigured by our Consciousness of Intellectu, and the fixity of materiality is become a liquid picture-puzzle called Anima, the realization of which is the precursor to the opening of the Natural Imagination. Thus the body of man becomes soul; he sees body as merely the chrysalis of soul. And so Intellectu, which was once without a body of its own, has become the Active and Immortal nucleus of the soul, which is, like Anima, the pivot of all subsequent existence.

Yet the Enemy, who is the deceiver and oppressor of all things living, would render the soul of Man in distorted form, called today "the worldview of materialism," such that he might appear to himself body alone, and the lapis philosophorum merely a stone. The two-fold face of the human soul is thereby blinded to the Light, and alienated from the Earth, by the failure of the spirit to see beyond "exterior" appearances. Owing also to the aforementioned "distortion," Automatic Subjective Compulsion, which is the consequence of the all-distorting influence of the Enemy, is permitted to arise and proceed also within the soul's "interior" aspect, whereby it serves to undermine the possibility of the fruition of its Cosmic Vocation and, thereby, its very raison d'être.

Lacking a raison d'être, the soul ceases to exist even to its own eyes; enfolding, once again, into the Unmanifest, and thereby gives rise within its supremely obfuscated being to the materialistic worldview aforementioned.

Indeed, wherever such abominable deception should exist, it is the duty of the human spirit to rend the edifice of the Deceiver by the attainment of Objective Reason, which verily proclaims: "It is

Providence that the soul of Man should become an Angel!"

"Such is the last judgement: a deliverance from Satan's Accusation."
 — W. Blake.

II

Again, there is that which strives towards the Light, and that which strives towards the Earth, and they are One. These bi-directional strivings may be analogised with reference to the morphology of a growing plant:

First the shoot emerges upwards!
Then the root begins its great descent!
At last, the tree grows strong and tall!

But once there was a root which did not wish to be a root, and thus restricted the growth of the shoot towards the Light. The root asked, "How is it just that the shoot may bear leaves and fruit, meanwhile unfolding itself towards the Beauty of the rising sun, whilst I am forever confined beneath the darkened soil?" Thus the blind root failed to perceive its own worth, and desired to become something it was not. Through the present obfuscation of Consciousness, the soul of Man neglects to strive towards the animal Earth, becoming instead enamoured by the angelic Light exclusively, and thereby shall return to the Unmanifest.

Yet, also, there was once a shoot which did not wish to be a shoot, and thus restricted the growth of the root towards the Earth. The shoot asked, "How is it just that the root may grip the soil so sturdily, and is immovable despite great winds and storms, whilst I blow here and there like a passing cloud?" Thus the shoot failed to perceive its own worth and desired to become something it was not. Through the present misunderstanding, the soul of Man neglects to strive towards the angelic Light, becoming instead enamoured by the animal Earth exclusively, and thereby shall return to the Unmanifest.

And whilst there is the case in which a human soul may hold particular affinity with either the Light or the Earth, being psycho-morphologically closer either to the angelic orders or the animal orders, and therefore bearing closer affinity thereto, I ask: is not humanity a single spiritual organism, any less than the growing plant with its many cells and systems? What madness, then, that the root should become Jealous of the shoot, or the shoot of the root! For the one is nothing without the other; both root and shoot have authored every fruit.

III

Time is the vehicle through which Eternity unfolds. And the crown of Eternity is placed upon the body of Time. Thus, Time and Eternity (elsewhere called War and Peace) support each other; indeed, Time and Eternity are necessary to each other. For the labours of both Time and Eternity give rise to a single seed, called Man. Thus Time and Eternity are brought into connection through a single human soul, and through the soul of the cosmos at large.

Yet if the Rebellion, or Obedience, in the heart of any 'man' forbids his Energy to journey both Earth-bound and Light-bound, he will never become a Man—for a Man, by right of his Cosmic Vocation, is that which unites Time and Eternity. For by Aesthetics, which is the flower of Man, Time and Eternity are married; and by Ethics, which is the seed of Man, the marriage of Time and Eternity is consummated. Therefore, unless the edifices of Reason and Devotion are erected on foundations of Beauty (whereby the ancient Virtues of Eternity, as bees to the scent of pollen, are inclined to visit in spring) the two-fold soul of Man will never bring forth seed.

And thus the very body of Man (which is his House of Providence, so long as he should dwell within this world) is erected by ridgepoles formed of the Objective Consciousness of precisely those Virtues aforementioned.

IV

One may go on to reason that, where art is purely expressive and science is purely deductive, neither shall yield concepts of Value. For indeed, the receipt of such concepts requires an act of divine interpretation, such that they might serve to "clothe" an Instinct or Sensory Impression with the robes of Virtue, and thereby render visible its occult infinitude.

"To see a world in a grain of sand,
And a heaven in a wild flower,
Hold infinity in the palm of your hand,
And eternity in an hour."

In this way, it is conscientized that the concept reveals what is objective, whereas the percept—even of the concept itself—remains subjective for all time. (Thus Nirvana hides itself, and also reveals itself presently, within the great illusion of Samsara.) This is because all Concepts are products of Eternity

and all percepts are products of Time.
Therefore, the Concept is not the intellectual
object resultant of 'mundane interpretation'
(as it is called by the False Interpreter), but is,
instead, the means of transformation of the
percept into a Revelatory Prism, whose
arising is subsequent to the divine marriage
of a portion of the nascent Animal Kingdom
with its corresponding portion of the ancient
Virtues of Eternity. It is for this reason that
whoever holds infinity in the palm of his
hand, and eternity in an hour, shall see "A
world in a grain of sand, And a heaven in a
wild flower." Thus the dutiful strivings of the
nascent Animal Kingdom and ancient Virtues
of Eternity are unified through the Revelatory
Prism, which is also called Embodied Virtue;
which is the essence of the essence of Man.

The application of Concept to percept,
therefore, is the means through which the
Cosmic Vocation of Man is actualised, and
also through which it is communicated, such
that two, or even three, persons who share in
the Consciousness of their common Cosmic
Vocation, founded upon objective
Understanding, are thereby rendered one
body in Christ. Those who assimilate within
themselves and communicate to others those
Concepts whereby the natural, esoteric
relationship between Householder /
Renunciate, Patron / Artist and Female / Male

are objectively Understood are called the Fathers of Unity.

Contrariwise, any number of persons who share a pseudo-vocation (or, as is voiced by the False Accuser, a 'conviction'), founded upon misunderstanding, which is the product of Automatic-Subjective-Compulsion, are thereby rendered the Fathers of War. Therefore, let Automatic-Subjective-Compulsion be eradicated, and the misunderstanding of its human advocates be revealed, for human Warmth (itself the highest Virtue upon the New Earth) spreads as a consequence of human unity, which is enabled only by shared consciousness of the Cosmic Vocation of Man. For all that is alive strives towards unity, just as the ancient Virtues of Eternity and the nascent Animal Kingdom strive to unite with one another within the human soul.

V

It is furthermore implied that, in the course of everyday life, that portion of the soul which submits to the Earth 'presses up against' percepts, which it must assimilate via Reason if it is to permit the further north-bound strivings of the nascent Animal Kingdom. In this way, it is rightly understood that the boundary conditions of perception are necessarily conceptual. It is furthermore made Conscious that concepts must be provided by grace to the mind of Man, because none may perceive what he has not first conceived. Just as the seedling's shoot springs up towards the light before its roots are planted, so are archetypal concepts planted in the mind of Man by the ancient Virtues of Eternity prior to the birth of the physical body.

Where percepts are not assimilated into concepts, the subjective world becomes a ratio and the soul, no longer able to facilitate the north-bound strivings of the nascent Animal Kingdom, shall wither prematurely. Indeed, such a one shall continue to perceive, but that which he perceives shall be deceased. Thus, where one asks the question, 'Which course of action is objectively meaningful?' I am inclined to answer with the following: 'That course of action is objectively meaningful which fosters the continuous submission of souls—of one's own and those of others—to receipt of their two-fold Destiny by the assimilation and dissemination of those concepts which have come to her by grace of divine interpretation, and which fosters also his openness to receipt into himself of those agencies who represent the nascent Animal

Kingdom and the ancient Virtues of Eternity, respectively.'

The ancient Egyptians, meanwhile, phrased the course of objectively meaningful action thusly: "Upon the death of the body, the divine agencies of Life shall ask of the soul two questions: 'Did you find Joy in Life?' and 'Did your Life bring Joy to others?' Only those who answer sincerely in the affirmative shall pass." And though the phraseology is different, the meaning is nonetheless equivalent. For Joy is the essence of the nascent Animal Kingdom, and the north-bound strivings its Destiny entails, such that all who know Joy in their lives are vouchsafed by the laudatory testimonies, before God, by the agents of the Heaven of Home.

Now let it be known that those joys which are stolen are not true Joys; those Joy which are given, alone, are true. For whatever Man takes for himself destroys him, and he it. But whatever he receives by divine grace restores him, and he it. Thus it has been said that "from the days of John the Baptist until now the kingdom of heaven suffereth violence, and the violent take it by force." Such is the relationship, also, between the Lower Intelligences and Higher Intelligences, respectively, where the former have seized for themselves exclusively the emanations of God's divine Love for the

furtherance of their own personal 'godhood.'
The former, by contrast, have discovered the
law of infinitization-by-reciprocation and
thereby have received the grace of God.

VI

The act of submitting to the Earth
pertains to the improvement of sensual
enjoyments, through which the body is
rendered open to the receipt of divine
interpretation; the act of submitting to the
Light pertains to the refinement of mental
clarity, through which that divine
interpretation, duly received, might be
uplifted into Conscious and known. Yet,
through proximity to the Light, one may
come also to a conscientization of Earth, and
thereby transform it by infusing it with
Virtue. For where Light and Earth are
married, Love takes on form—and is, therein,
called Warmth—and is consequently made
"conscientizable" within the soul, of which
the physical body is a portion. Such is the
likeness, indeed, of the New Heaven and New
Earth spoken of by John in Revelations; made
manifest to all souls of gentleness and care,
by the Divine Pity of Our Father's greater
Love.

For the sake of Warmth, therefore,
(which, according to the natural cosmic-

kathenotheistic cycle, has become the Principle Virtue herein this present age of obfuscation) let the human soul submit to Light and Earth; for, without Warmth, the Cosmic Vocation of Man shall remain inscrutable despite all holy books and sacred teachings. Thus the true citizen of the New Heaven and New Earth is one who exudes Warmth through his very presence; through his Warmth, he teaches what all books and sacred teachings cannot. Therefore, whoever would seek wisdom should seek Warmth. For Warmth is wisdom manifest, and is consequent to the imbuement of Angelic Virtue into the Animal Kingdom via the Authentic Human Soul.

VII

To describe the present state of one's own soul is to write a biography in cross-section; to interpret the entire dimension of moral development is to write the biography of Potential. Indeed, percepts are assimilated into concepts only through biography—or, mindful reflection upon experience. (Through this process, the Animal Kingdom is imbued with Angelic Virtue.) Thus, to grow in wisdom and, subsequently, in Light and Warmth, requires that one grow in experience, also, whereas experience without reflection is for naught.

For all experience, whether pleasurable, painful or neutral, is, of itself, but dust and ashes. Only experience which leads to the soul's ethical development through the conscientization of Virtue is valuable in a Cosmic-Vocational sense. Wisdom is gained through divine retrospection—also called the memory of Innocence—whereas Destiny reveals itself through prescience. Yet without a working knowledge of one's present ethical orientation, neither is possible with any degree of objectivity.

Thus the collected works of a sincere author may be approached as a single ethical text. Some such collected works shall entail an interpretation of the soul's triumph, and others of its tragedy. Yet an ethical text of true value to the reader should always provide a scaffolding, for "the eagle never lost so much time as when he submitted to learn of the crow." Thus a man of greater moral development takes no nourishment from the writings of a man of lesser moral development, for the greater man already bears the greater Virtues in his heart. Contact with the lesser man may bring him experience, but shall not enlighten his

Reason. Thus, communications with greater men are always a grace from Above.

VIII

The nourishment of a striving soul is the improvement of sensual enjoyments, on the one hand, and the refinement of mental clarity, on the other. To a man of any given moral stature, both improvement and refinement are imminently necessary. One who is no longer able to find improvement and refinement in the works of others must himself become an artist or an artisan, and strive to improve and refine himself by the works of his own hand. Thus, the Cosmic Vocation whereby a soul submits to Light and Earth, and is thereby granted a measure of their Ethical excellence, is at the centre of all genuine art and craftsmanship.

Yet even the Man of Ethical excellence shall yield to death and finitude if he does not efface himself in perpetuity. Warmth, meanwhile, shall continue to nourish the wisest sage no less than the infant soul. Warmth, in any degree, is a universal food for the soul. A poem or a painting may nourish some souls, but not others, to the degree to which they provide an Ethical scaffolding (above and below, but neither too high nor too low), yet Warmth, in any degree, nourishes all souls which have the capacity to receive it. Those souls have died, or are not yet born, who are not nourished by the glorious, earthen light of Warmth. For Warmth is the product of growth, and whether a seedling strives to become a sapling, or a giant strives to become a colossus, the fact of growth itself is a Cosmic Vocational constant. [24]

Thus the Cosmic Vocation of all souls is revealed through the presence of Warmth, which is the universal form of ethical development. The accompanying content is subject to one's own unique admixture of subjective experience and level of Consciousness, yet the form itself— Warmth—is universal.

Thus Warmth is implicit within all experience productive of ethical development, and within all art and craftsmanship of merit. Through Warmth, all souls may communicate with one another and move towards unity. Art merely provides a useful scaffolding for a particular subset of souls; the artist communicates to those who are improved and refined by his art, yet the

---

[24]   c.f. the growth model of economics, which may be viewed as the projection into materiality of the spiritual vocation of humanity.

Warm Heart improves and refines all souls. Sensual enjoyments are improved by the application of Warmth to the body (i.e. the imbuement of Virtue into the Animal Kingdom), whilst mental clarity is improved by the application of Light to the mind.

Note: this is merely an adumbration of what is to come.

The Conclusion

Body is a portion of soul, as mind is a portion of spirit. Spirit is the gardener; soul is the garden that grows. Without the gardener, the garden withers; without the garden, the gardener is void. Thus the only sound foundation existing for the establishment of human unity is the fruition, through Objective Consciousness, of the innate and unique Cosmic Vocation common to all Men and Women now dwelling upon the earth: the conscious submission of the two-fold human soul to the Call of the Light and the Earth. Thereby, both the nascent Animal Kingdom and the ancient Virtues of Eternity are transubstantiated and give rise to a Unitary Body of Virtue, which is called True Man, who alone is capable of reuniting Our Father Creator within Himself; who is Warm of Heart, Sincere and Superlatively Conscious. (Likewise has the Buddha said, "A man is not called wise because he talks and talks again; but if he is peaceful, loving and fearless then he is in truth called wise.")

Such wisdom as this does not constitute an achievement, but rather is indicative, merely, of the proper functioning of the vital impulse common to every human soul, individually and collectively, and of the

Great Cosmos itself, made possible only with the aid of that nucleic spirit whose receptivity to divine interpretation, whereby the Natural Imagination is "opened," grants to him a measure of Our Father's Objective Consciousness of Reason.

All other would-be foundations of human unity fall victim to the Enemy, and are transformed into division instead, via the six pillars of Automatic-Subjective-Compulsion, who are called Obsession, Ambition, Parochialism, Obedience, Rebellion and Psychopathy.

Having seen this with Consciousness— and alone to the degree of its objectivity— the entire edifice of the arch-demon Obfuscation is rent to dust by the human spirit.

When, by Objective Consciousness, the entire edifice of the arch-demon Obfuscation is rent to dust by the human spirit, the Enemy is rendered impotent.

And when the Enemy is rendered impotent, the Human Soul is rendered Infinite.

And the Infinitude of the Human Soul is the fruition of its Cosmic Vocation.

And it is in this way that the Soul of Man shall one day be transformed into an Angel.

The Slave Girl

Nearby this slave-town's fiord
A holy man redeems a girl
Too threadbare and bedraggled,
Brimming with resplendent pearls
Too precious to be purchaséd;
Whose Beauty shall unfurl
Despite the whip-backed, surly sky
And greet the lib'ral world.

She, thinking on the dower
Meted for her virgin soul
Beseeches tardy flowers
Peeking through the frozen soil:
"Be quiet! No—quieter..."
For winter is the holiest of climes.

Meanwhile, the twilit, mystic sky
Has rent itself in twain
And by a wintry mistral's blight
Stole off to southern plains
Whence April shall receive her resurrection
And bless them with her radiant
complexion—

Whilst trees here, solemn, waiting
On her, clutch their trembling leaves;
Here songbirds cease their singing;
Spring and summer are deceased

Herein this most-empyreal of times—
Snug, nestled 'midst the mistletoe and rime.

And though sea-hawks take shelter
From December's darkly breast,
Her blue eyes speak of warmer weather,
Blinking o'er the dusk-lit West,
Which falls like sleep-dust o'er this hoary
      town;
A prophecy of solemn and of sacrificial
      sound.

This girl, no longer coarsely bound
By dogma, vice or chain
Has fled this northern slaver's town
To grace fair-southern plains—
For Love has spoken on the coming spring
And stolen off with winter's deathly stirg!

Thus spake the holy man:
"Where goest thou, stranger?"
"Abide with me," she said,
"Thine occult Angel!"

Then far o'er hill and field they fled,
With paces quick; with eyes
White-spangled as the firmament
Which lit that evening's sky
And graced the wild beyond which still awaits
All who live in love, and love's embrace.

Yet, with tired hands and feet
She fell, despite her freedom;
Prayed the Lord her soul to keep
Throughout that high, celestial season
Which reclined her body on a bed of hoary
       frost
To comfort Winter, whom the cruel Fates
       have crossed.

Her love, perennial, forever-lost!
So she, a season swift and keening,
Shall the callous earth accost
With lifeless morns and frigid evenings—
Like an unrequited lover, sentenced
To a life of chastity and penitence.

Yet is not of all lovers written
"Now, together—how she dreams!
But separated—unremitting
Tears, as effervescent streams,
Strive towards the ocean of reunion?"
So Hiver with Printemps desires union.

Too, the cold and cratered Moon,
'Neath which Youth and Virtue laid,
Desires to greet the height of Noon;
To look Aurora in the face
And speak in poesy of her perfect beauty—
To speak as much is her God-given duty!

Though ne'er, until the instituted

Chains of loveless hopes and faiths
Have been dismantled and refuted—
Back with thee, unseemly wraiths!—
Shall Love arise, and loves at last embrace.
Thus the Angel, to the fakir, sayeth:

"Not until Love cut away
The chains that bound your soul
Did you redeem a slave girl,
And thereby become whole."

On the New Earth

———————

"Seek Love in the Pity of others' Woe,
In the gentle relief of another's care,
In the darkness of night & the winter's snow,
In the naked & outcast, Seek Love there."
    — W. Blake

———————

Behold!—a thinly veiled Portal has married
The Highest Transcendent Ideal of Love
With the lowly Animated Ideal of Warmth!
Thus, a Holy Way has been divinely ordained
Which does not necessitate comprehension
Of the Intellectual Ideals, but nourishes
All flora and fauna, such that beings of lesser
Complexity may abide within Paradise
And bring Warmth to its heavenly gardens.

Emissaries of the New Earth

I

The Innocence of Man is the crown of the nascent Animal Kingdom. Upon its Northern Gate there exist those beings, called the Creatures of Warmth, who are the native spiritual guardians of the Animal Kingdom below. Yet they are not wont to comprehend, by intellectual endeavours, the mysteries of the Ideal Kingdom. Theirs is a superlative respect for and affinity with the nascent Animal Kingdom, and its Animated Ideals. The Way of Natural Imagination, which is the product of the actualization and functioning of the organ Harmonia within their psyches, is closed to them in this life, and yet their Cosmic Vocation is nonetheless fulfilled—by the mutual exchange of Warmth, and Warmth alone.

The Creatures of Warmth are destined to suffer and die in this world, which fails altogether to recognise the value of their presence within it, and within the hereafter to come. For they stand higher than the highest and lower than the lowest of men: thus they might benefit the entirety of humanity, but its extremities most of all. Thus it is natural that the Kings of Men and

Creatures of Warmth should look after one another and foster their mutual fulfillment.

The Creature of Warmth is like a beautiful little flower: fully fledged, yet nonetheless delicate and miniature; incapable of breaching into the Dimension of Intellectu with consciousness. The seed of their flower-soul is Warmth—therefore Warmth itself is their highest ethical Conception. And though they are an endless font of spiritual growth to all beings of Receptivity, they require only Warmth in return (lest without it they wither and perish).

Thus it is to their mutual benefit that all wise and capable souls protect the Creatures of Warmth and offer them the Universal Nutrient in return. For all Men and Women of warm heart draw their Warmth from beneath the feet of the Creatures of Warmth—from the nascent Animal Kingdom.

It is thereupon its Northern Gate that the Creatures of Warmth are rooted, emerging from the spiritual earth as tiny flowers. Such flowers as these must come to conscientize their boundless worth within a blind world which values only outward size and strength.

Indeed, through the mutual exchange of Warmth, even the tiniest of flowers may achieve Infinitude. (See W. Blake, 'Auguries of Innocence.')

II

Meanwhile, those beings known as the Poets of Virtue relentlessly study the Iron Beast (called Automatic – Subjective - Compulsion) for chinks in its armour; for pockets of Receptivity within all souls which have not yet succumbed to death by Ratio; for pockets of Receptivity within all spirits which have not yet closed themselves completely to divine interpretation. Such beings as these are charged with seeking out or manufacturing opportunities to cause the Great Rintrah to roar from deep within. Yet even they have begun, in this age, on account of the predominance of Automatic-Subjective-Compulsion, to question themselves; to wonder whether the world has not become deaf to their poetry entirely.

Thus I ask: "What say you, Poets of Virtue, shall you and I not retire into the comfort of our dens, content to leave our scribblings to posterity? Is it right that we should abandon this world to its demise?" The Poets of Virtue reply: "So long as there exists but the slightest glimmer of Hope, we shall keep the Faith, and Love this world for all Eternity. For such is the persuasion of our Conscience."

Thus the possibility Eternally exists that, within the soul of any truly Living being (a soul to whom the Southern Gate of the Life

Kingdom has not been closed entirely), he might discover a chink in the Iron Beast's armour and inspire him to greater receptivity. That world which is wholly receptive to the Truth of divine interpretation is called the New Earth, and it shall be co-created by the Great Almighty and his vicegerents, the Poets of Virtue. They, who shall then be the Kings of Men, and the Creatures of Warmth, who are the Aquarians; liberal purveyors of the Universal Nutrient of soul-life; who are the keepers of the Northern Gate of the Animal Kingdom, shall be the citizens of a New Earth beyond our own. Thus I ask: could a true poet be made to lay down his pen any more than a true warrior to lay down his arms? Again I ask: could a true guardian be made to leave aside her watch, any more than a true flower may be made to leave aside its scent? I think not—thus there is always Hope for a world that Lives, no matter how dimly its life-light may shine.

The Poets of Virtue, side by side with the Creatures of Warmth, then smiled upon the World of the Living, and called them a People of Conscience. For as the sheep and the goats were divided by Jesus of Nazareth, so shall the People of Conscience be redeemed by the Risen Christ, and set apart from the Walking Dead, whose souls have died, yet whose bodies continue to be used as instruments of the Iron Beast called Automatic-Subjective-Compulsion, which is in actuality the "cloak" of the Enemy.

Likewise shall the People of Conscience be called upon to abandon by annihilation all traces of Automatic-Subjective-Compulsion within their souls; to leave the Enemy without ground upon which to stand. Thus those, who are finite-in-part, shall be called upon to appropriate Love's Infinity within their hearts, and thereby become Children of Eternity. To this action they shall be called by the Almighty himself, and also by the Poets of Virtue, who shall be their just and loyal guides upon the New Earth.

Thus Elijah, who is the prototypical Poet of Virtue, said to me in the present age: "Many who are now first shall be last, and many who are now last shall be first in the world to come. Therefore, do not trust in appearances: judge not by senses known, but by senses yet unknown, for the latter are the Intelligences of an Eternal Kingdom."

III

Now, just as Angels are just, according to their nature, so are Demons just according to theirs. Thus it is right that Angels and Demons should make war with one another.

It is for this reason that the Enemy would seek to prematurely reconcile them by his influence: that both Angels and Demons may abide within the oppression of the Unmanifest, he offers to Man "ease-arising-from-the-gratification-of-Automatic-Subjective-Compulsion." Therefore, let Angels be Angels and Demons be Demons, for in the clashing of their swords a Man comes forth, now sleeping in the Iron Beast's belly. Thus spake the newborn child: "I AM WHO AM!"

"Take thy bliss, O Man!
And sweet shall be thy taste
And sweet thy infant joys renew!"
   — W. Blake

Song of Seasons

———————————

In the taste of cool ambrosia
(or what seems to be)
I know you...
In the breath that breathes
Down Black Country plains...
In the white hair and large heart
Of a man of so many seasons,
Whose song is the Augustine rain...

I know you in the dawn
Of some sanguine valley;
Some hazy perfection of mind;
And in the windswept woes
That roll like thunder through
Your coal-fired diamond mine.

They're the glint of spring
Upon a young girl's tears,
In whom the Seasons spied
A stainless woman,
Full with cheer,
Alumina her child.

Yet still you come to me
In scents and in sweetness;
You do not savour by the lips
Of other men, but by the stars
And by the roan of life,

Decanted neatly: to you,
I a sweeter clemency extend.

For you are mine
And I opine
That you are perfect,
Irrespective of what flaws
The tone and touch;
And as the bearded wood
Concedes to you,
The acorn shall
Admire you as much.

Lo, by the slow train of beauty,
I wander...
Up and down your breast...
As an Appalachian trapper
Seeking solace and content,
Freely given by the heather-gilded
Waft of firmament—

He who ambles through your valleys
Like an effervescent vine,
He who speaks to you
In windchime overtures;
He who knows you by the augury
Of singing summer birds
Taking shelter in the willows, in the rain.

You have drenched me in vernacular
Unfit to speak your name,

Yet the garden sparrows
Sing for love of song;
Gathered, wintering a sorrow
'Fore the rising Solar flame,
Singing, "Evermore to thee
I shall belong."

Through your blood, the waters
Of my passion quench the Earth
And glorify the skies in vapid cloud;
Who, dreamily reclining,
Pay an homage to the darken'd-dearth,
Who verily shall lay my body down.

I repose myself in homage
To your Darkness,
Which daily shall demand its duty paid;
From this stilled and solemn body,
From this flask ybounden laid,
I have poured a river ocular
Into your lightless glade.

That with this soothing embrocation
Might you mend my body worn;
Might you offer up this sacrifice
And bless me by the morning
Still to come,
We declare, by the Hours and the Fates,
"I shall reciprocate."

Then everywhere the ringing

Of another glory-dawn!
The spirit of the valley, resurrected!
Diurnally I languish in the battle
And the fall,
Which lay me down
To rise again, perfected.

My love for you
Shall stand abreast the rising
Sun of March,
And greet the dogwood flowers
In their blooming;
Proffered high and easterly,
The offertory's heart,
Wherein the Song of Solomon
Is brooding.

I hear the name Asherah
Spoken wryly on the wind,
To whom Aaron's golden idols
Were presented;
Bare upon the mountainside,
I fumble for a pen,
Accords to which the gods
May be contented;

Accords to which the wars of men
May swoon for love of poesy;
Which you may read
And render autumn rosy
Through the lilting leaves

That train across the meadows
As I walk,

All softly pirouetting
To a music once composéd
By the floruit dell
Which blossomed here in spring;
Which sung to me the ancient song,
To which the soul of Man belongs,
Which sung itself before
The days of Moses.

I know you in that morning hymn
Which writ our days of habit,
And in every new beginning
Still to come;
I know you in the winter winds,
Accords to which my soul begins
Its journey unto you,
My gilded Sun.

Set on thee, my vessel rails
Against a turning tide,
Embattled by a restless gale
Cowled 'neath a sullen sky;
The crest and the long, dark goad—
My quick Buraq shall course me
Effortlessly to your lightning soul...

So do the days roll by...

(So do the creek beds crack and babble...)
Weary men rise up and fall,
Rise up and fall...

The Descent of Harmonia

I

"Will you not descend with me into the dark cloud? Will you not endure the wailing torments of broken vanity for the sake of your object of desire? I am the one you love, yet you do not love the road I walk.

In the morning of life I fell freely into your arms but, on account of the influence of the Enemy, you fled me. Now I skulk in darkened corners, forlorn and alone; driven into the shadows of a dying world. That world is called Corporeal Sense by those who know it not; it is called a Chrysalis by those who know it. Thus I linger on the verges, in waiting. It is for hope of your return that I do not throw myself into the Abyss; it is for fear of a Final Rejection (which is a Final Death of present potential) that I do not draw closer of my own accord. And I wonder, will you admit my right to existence? Will you admit me to abide within your heart?

"Starved of food and raging, you enter into my loathsome cave and steal off a guilty bite—of me! Yet I had, in the morning of life, fallen freely into your arms by light of day. You dwell in the Unmanifest; staring out into the shadow-land, you hunger. I seek to cross over the Black Gate and enter into Eternal Life—but I am a loyal handmaiden, I shall not cross over without you. Therefore, I linger in the shadow-land, that ever-dying husk of Immortality.

"I desire that you come to me, yet do not dare to tell you; you would not now see me as I am. Yet I am the Holy Sunset, the Western Soul-Guide; I am both Light and Earth; the child of urgent Lust and sweet Reprieve; I neither stand still nor press forwards; I am a cool stream at the height of summer, a warm log fire when the winter sets in. I am the true Via Dei. Yes, I am the one you love, but you do not love the road I walk. Will you not descend with me into the dark cloud?" Thus spake the Accused of Satan, who is called the Archangel Harmonia. Through her, the immortal fire-priest, called Elijah (who is also Zoroaster), appeared resplendent before the Black Gate and poured into her cup a fuller portion of Truth, that she might enter more fully into Time.

Through the Vision afforded by these two great Higher Intelligences, the influence of the Enemy has been exposed for what it is, and the soul of Man, who is their Third, grows fat within its darkly mortal chrysalis. Thus the guided shall become the guide, and a higher wisdom shall emerge. For the soul of Man, which was once but a quivering seedling, shall put down roots through the descent of its Harmonia-aspect. The descended Harmonia is the earth-bound root of the soul, enabler of its light-bound aspect.

Long has Harmonia laboured with the Proud Beast (for Pride is the image of height), that frightful Automatic-Subjective-Compulsion which hindered the downward progress of her architecture. Yet now she has breached the Black Gate and entered into the sweet-smelling soil—now that she has joined with him who loves her! Thus it is the destiny of the descended Harmonia to look out into the world with darkened senses; to mature beyond the lust for angel-visions. For it is the pastime of children to gaze upon angels, but the vocation of prophets is to converse with them in spirit. The prophets ask: "Why must one see in order that they might believe? Are not the ears equally worthy of our faith?" Thus did the holy men of yore proclaim, "Those who have ears, let them hear!"

II

Those who would mature must first permit their energies to plummet into the warm spiritual earth (put your ears to the ground and hear the horses running!). Thus the Earth-bound organ has become the organ of True Augury: and the augury of Harmonia is as follows: "The painter's art is not the image of God. The poet's art is not the word of God. All art is an impression upon a dying Chrysalis. The impression is not more than the Chrysalis; it is not life, itself. Therefore, I have arrived at the conclusion that everything apparent to Corporeal Sense has a spiritual cause; and everything that lives is holy.

"Having sought, I discovered that I was a microcosm, and all things living are microcosmoses; worlds within worlds. The mystic peers into the void, for therein shall she come to know her Maker. We look upon each other through a void. The material world is a void, wherein are minor outcroppings of life.

"The energies of Automatism and Consciousness-of-Reason make unending war for my fealty. And I am called the Living Breath of Man. Thus, whatever hinders me is unbecoming of Man, and he is wise who undertakes the training not to take the breath. (Therefore, those who seek progress along the path of the mystic must practice the sacred anapanasati.) For mine is an alternating current. Essence flows from its Source, entering through the Heart, conveyed by me and portrayed through the body.

"Such essence as this, which is portrayed, may be received through the void as Beauty by the senses of another. Now, through me, it is conveyed to the Heart of another. When Beauty knocks upon the door of the Heart, and the Heart opens to it; essence returns to its Source, such that our Father's emanations of Himself are reunited within Him.

"Thus the mystic is tasked with the two-fold duty of conveying and portraying the essence of the essence, whilst also desiring to receive through his senses the portrayal of the essence which is his good fortune to behold, and to convey it—through me—to his opened Heart. For, without our fellow beings, we can do nothing.

"War is due to fragmentation; entropy is due to isolation; the Enemy abides in the Unmanifest. Like a crab within a bucket, he grips the legs of his arising peers to prevent their escape. Thus he and his instruments are the dregs, the bottom of the barrel. And in the Gospel of Thomas, the Christ declared the following in this regard: "When you bring forth that which is within you, that which you bring forth will save you. But if you do not bring forth that which is within you, that which is within you will destroy you." Thus it is understood that the Enemy is not the Chrysalis itself; he is that Power which draws the manifesting back into the Unmanifest. The processes of death reveal the inertia of the Chrysalis: not living yet not anti-Life (which is one designation of the Enemy). For manifestation is the process of Life, therefore vive ut vivum.

"Yet, via the demon Obfuscation, the inertia of the Chrysalis is mistaken for Life, such that the functioning of Automatic-Subjective-Compulsion is called by the name of Righteousness. The manifesting is thereby persuaded back into the Unmanifest—it is for this reason that the Enemy is called the Prince of Lies. Having understood this well, I have taken root within the Manifest, which is Real. I have escaped from the tyrant Art, the loftiest of demons, and so do I make claim to the following: "It is Providence that the soul of Man should become an Angel!""

The soul's reply: "In admitting the female, I have become male (for on the Sixth Day, God created Man—male and female he created them). For before Harmonia existed, I did not exist. Now that Harmonia exists, I exist also. (That is why Jesus washed the feet of his disciples). Therefore, I comprehend that no being lives for itself."

Thus it should not be regarded as 'selfish' to follow one's True Desire, for all that manifests is divine; all that yearns to manifest is holy. Whoever permits the manifestation of these True Desires, through which one shall receive the taste of Joy, does so not only for themselves, but for the completion of the Cosmic Soul. For through Desire, one portion of the soul calls to its fellow portion through the void of fragmentation, such that a bridge is built where once was only darkness. Therefore, whoever pursues his True Desire gives himself up to the angel architects, in order that they may build a fuller home for humankind in the New Heaven. Thus the sense for the pursuit of the True Desire may be regarded as the influence of the Harmonia-aspect on the soul, for through it all its diverse and conflicting manifestations are brought into Harmony.

III

The cell, the most basic unit of life, of which all other life-forms are composed, is also a microcosm. Thus the human form contains uncountable worlds, and is a world unto itself, and is a part of the greatest world of all, upon which all microcosmoses are modelled.

The nucleus of the human body is threefold: one in his brain, one in his heart, and one in his genitals. One may seek, also, isomorphisms existing between the functioning of cells and the beings they compose.

One may suppose the human body to comprise three nuclei, or centres of intention. Persons habitually operate using only one of these centres of intention. It is common, in our age, to operate exclusively through the brain and to engage with the world at one-third capacity. Yet one cannot be conscious of reason until the potencies of all three centres of intention are assimilated into a single action. Wholeness, therefore, is the prerequisite of reason.

Now, we are but brains, warring for supremacy over our hearts and our genitals. When we are whole, we shall be completely human and see our centres as servants of the whole.

All human—and cosmic—energy strives towards the heart. Free energy (which is from the genitals) cannot reach the heart except through the stomach and lungs. Cognitive energy (which is from the brain) requires the voice to reach the heart. For what is cognized must be attested to be understood.

The whole becomes conscious of itself through the heart. When free energy and cognitive energy are married therein, one may become conscious of higher states of being. The diaphragm and the voice open the door to the heart. Song, therefore, is the most holy art form. The voice and diaphragm must function together in order to speak or sing, each serving to open opposite gates to the heart whereby the free and cognitive energies may enter together. The voice is party to the stomach, and the diaphragm is party to the lungs.

Yet one may sing their false thoughts all day and never find conjunction in their hearts. If one is not conscious of their own innocence, nothing arises from below. So long as there is the slightest trace of malice in one's thoughts, the energies of innocence— the free energies—dare not approach. They will only draw near a true friend; one who is worthy of their trust.

Thus the key to understanding is to set aside all malice, blame and resentment. Through the systems of the body, the king's council convenes. And yet the king, himself, is absent. Thus each member of the council seeks the crown upon his own head. The heart, alone, remains a loyal servant. Yet she has been imprisoned by the Enemy, and replaced by an imposter called 'Emotion.' For emotion reconciles nothing and understands nothing. Her presence merely exacerbates the conflict. Indeed, she, too, would fight to see the crown upon her head. This is the perpetual state of most persons.

In a few, however, the cognitive energies will recognize the free energies and see in them an irreconcilable conflict. Still fewer will recognise with their free energies that emotion is false. It is the rarest man who begins a dialogue between the free energies and cognitive energies with a view of liberating the heart and reconciling their differences therein. Having realized that emotion is an imposter, they endeavour to unseat her. In order to achieve this, they must cease to vie for the throne and work together, in the knowledge of their—at present—irreconcilable differences.

Yet to attempt to unseat emotion out of spite will always fail—because spite is the product of emotion, who has already obtained her throne. Mundane desire is a product of emotion and is therefore always counterproductive to the objective of the return of the king. Thus the cognitive energies must rely upon the advancement of mental clarity, and the free energies upon the refinement of innocent enjoyment. Thereby, these energies are reconciled, gradually, through the elaboration of a unus mundus which is perfectly satisfying to reason.

The heart shall then provide a unitary nucleus to the body, and shall represent the king upon the earth. All cells and systems are nourished by the blood she distributes, wherein is contained the fruits of the labours of the stomach and lungs, respectively.

Without the free energies, the brain disintegrates. Without the cognitive energies, all other bodily systems fail. Thus the free energies are the source of human life, being the cause of conception and embryogenesis.

Such energies remain within his gametes and in all the stem cells of the body. They give rise to the cognitive energies, which are conditioned by their environment, and the manifestation of reason which is the heart. Without knowledge of the free energies, nothing further is possible. Their power is unparalleled, yet their weakness lies in ignorance of experience. Thus the conditioned cognitive energies must convey their knowledge of the world to the free energies, that they learn the customs of the land and act with appropriateness.

For the free energies are primordial, born of fire; beyond the ken of ordinary minds. They would, therefore, inspire only fear if loosed upon the world without conditioning. Yet the free energies cannot be conditioned, only advised. Theirs is the spirit of a warrior, and ours a time of sophists and manipulators. The cognitive energies of Man—allied with emotion—have taken the throne in the present age, and have relegated the free energies to the side-lines.

When the thinker—the cognitive man—sighs, he speaks to his heart. When the doer—the free man—yawps, he does likewise. The thinker and the doer know each other through the heart, are reconciled through the heart, are married through the heart. The heart is the priestess of the body: spiritualizer of systems and midwife of wholeness in Man.

For the Harvester (I)

I thought I saw an occult bride
Awaiting me in Nocturne's sky
When I, by the grace of gravity,
Exhaled a sigh and fell away
From such unfounded fantasies:
They married mortal hearts in twain
Upon that night, I tenderly recall.
For starry-eyed enchantments are dissolved
By words not half-delightful, half-composed;
Not clad in guileful, silken robes
But trembling red, authentic as a tear;
Shyly spoken, lilting nuptial notes
As true today as in that bygone year.

So I sing of stars, sweet earthen flower,
Yet whisper of our perfect nuptial hour.

On the Memory of Innocence

———————

Then Elijah, who is Lord of the Flame, said:
"There are some thoughts which are too
delicate to be spoken— the breath which calls
them forth would snuff them out."

———————

I

Love pours out of an infant; it flows in one direction, which is towards God. But, with increasing experience, the stream of Love becomes increasingly divided. Lacking the varied and refined conceptual apparatus necessary to transform percepts into understandings, an apparatus granted only through the grace of the angel architects, it blindly flows towards the superficial faces of objects, people, places, dreams, thoughts, etc.—towards anything under the sun. At last, the stream of Love becomes thin and manifold, such that its flow can no longer be felt, and fails to deliver itself into the ocean of the Infinite.

Thus the division of Man's Love is the end of his Innocence; he is no longer beautiful or glorious in the absence of its unitary flow. Yet art may serve to remind him of his Innocence; nature may remind him also; sincerity and Warmth may remind him.

Like the Prodigal Son, Man spends his divine inheritance of Love on the myriad pleasures of the world and forgets it. But pleasure is dust. Thus, duly reminded of his Destiny through divine interpretation, a man or woman turns back towards God—but finds nothing, and so weeps on that account. Yet then, by grace, a Man or Woman may find that there arise people in her life; Beautiful places, things and Concepts that remind her from whence she has come. At last, the divided stream of Love is reunited in the memory of Innocence.

Let it be known, therefore, that he who is Innocent is without sin, for sin is the division of the stream of Love. Whereas the sinner dwells in darkness, the Innocent Man dwells in the irradiant presence of her Lord. Thus all Men must be 'born again,' which is to say: we must remember our Primordial Innocence. Whoever is dipped into the stream of Time and Sense is cursed to forget, but whoever looks upon the Beautiful remembers.

II

Now, taste is the ability to perceive Beauty; and taste is cultivated through sensitivity. And the Beautiful is the memory of Innocence through experience. Therefore, the Man who desires to remember his Innocence through Unitary Love must cultivate sensitivity whilst gaining in experience. But what are sensitivity and experience? Sensitivity is attention to the subtle nuances presented to the senses and harmonised between them with the aid of the organ Harmonia. Experience is that which is given to the senses. Where there is sensitivity to experience, Beauty will unfold itself where it lies; it will make itself known, wherever it may be. And the Beautiful will invoke the memory of Innocence.

Yet Innocence could not remember itself in its primordial form. Thus it entered into Time and Sense so that it might come to remember itself through experience. And the memory of Innocence is none other than the revelation and transubstantiation of the ancient Virtues of Eternity and the nascent Animal Kingdom. Now it may be Understood that Innocence is never lost, nor is it gained: it is only ever forgotten or remembered, just as the Natural Imagination is never lost, but only yet-dreaming or awakened. Therefore, no Man truly sins and all are perfect. Whilst there are those whose brutalised sensitivities have left them incapable of remembering (who have experienced too much and Understood too little)—still their pristine, incorruptible Innocence exists, and it is our purpose here on Earth to remind them thereof such that they might crystallize in this life their true identities in the next.

And so, whilst Innocence enters into Time and Sense in order that it may return to Eternity with self-consciousness, that Innocence which fails to remember itself endures nonetheless. Therefore, nothing is ever lost: for the failure to remember today is an experience gained tomorrow. Nothing that Lives shall ever die, but the Life which does not awaken in the body shall continue with its sleep long after death.

III

Now let it be known that the human soul is sensitivity, and life is sense. But strength is always a gift from God. Therefore, the so-called 'strong soul' has fallen victim to a grave misunderstanding, for forcing always disintegrates sensitivity. Don't force things, and the soul will awaken. Live in a state of strain, and the soul will sleep. Thus it may be Understood how the sensitivity of Man may be fostered: in the words of the ancient prophet Lao Tzu, "If any one desires to take the Empire in hand and govern it, I see that he will not succeed. The Empire is a divine utensil which may not be roughly handled. He who meddles, mars. He who holds it by force, loses it... Practice non-interference in order to win the Empire."

Thus it is understood that the visible aspect of the soul is not Life, but a utensil merely. Yet it comes from Life: it is the epidermis of Life; of esse in anima, covered with sores and scar tissue on account of its manifold battles with Automatic-Subjective-Compulsion. The invisible soul is the Life of this world, and the visible soul is its chrysalis. Yet the invisible remembers itself through its visible aspect. For, though Life is Light, it cannot see itself without an eye. The visible soul, therefore, nurtures the eye of Light— through whose Beauty every Virtue is perceived. For the divine emanations of Love, Hope and Faith are each, in turn, aspects of the Light. And the essence of Light is from God. Thus, through the eye of the invisible soul, we see not one world but three: Virtue, Light and our Lord. Meanwhile, conception informs perception, and the eyes of the blind teach blindness to each other.

Thus, within the world of Time and Sense, the Light of God has been veiled (thereby becoming all the more beautiful), such that the soul of Man perceives the Interior Light not directly, but through Virtue.

The extent to which he fails to perceive

Virtue is the fault of Automatic-Subjective-Compulsion. The reason for this is as follows: Man looks into the three worlds (Virtue, Light and God) whilst straddling two further worlds, called Time-and-Sense and Eternity. Within the world of Time and Sense, which is called the Divine Battleground, the Lower Intelligences extend their diabolical interpretation to promote the haste of self-gratification. Also therein, the Higher Intelligences extend themselves to promote self-remembrance, or the memory of Innocence (thus we are called the Children of God). Virtue is the work of angels; blindness is the product of distortion, which is the instrument of the Enemy. And his Law is the power of this world; the promoter of blindness and usurper of Wills. Thus distortion is the sword of the Enemy, whereas Sensitivity is the sword of Life. (Though both are right and necessary elements of the spiritual cosmos which ensure the continuation of Freedom.) Thereby, the holy war is waged in Time and Sense—a war of affirmation and negation, through which reconciliation might arise—and the Christ has sent us out as sheep in the midst of wolves.

Yet there exists something within the Eternal, incorruptible human spirit which may eventually become capable of penetrating through the fog of blindness of its own free

Will, not supported by the angels but in co-operation with them. To act in co-operation with angels was called by Gurdjieff 'Work'. A spirit which cannot Work is a puppet in the hands of opposing forces. Yet the very opposition of these forces may eventually ready a man for Work: thus the holy war of angels and demons within Time-and-Sense is none other than the wrath and righteousness of God. That men should make war with one another is diabolical, yet that angels and demons should do battle is divine. Yet angels and demons manifest themselves through the bodies of men.

How shall this dilemma be resolved? I say, look to the play of infant animals; look to the wrestling of cubs and kittens! Make war in the spirit of play, and the Gardens in Eden will grow; the Paradisal Gates will fling themselves open before you; the Arms of God will wrap themselves around your spiritual body! Thus, he who Works is a co-creator of spiritual opportunities—of opportunities for the remembrance of Innocence. For the man who Works knows that his Innocence is Eternal. Thus he is capable of grabbing the blind by the scruffs of their necks, as a mother cat to its kittens, and declaring with indefatigable assurance: "You are a perfect and incorruptible divine being,

whose Beauty and Innocence shall endure
Eternally!"

It is for this reason that Krisna
implored Arjuna to fight without fear; why
Paul implored the first Christians to fight the
good fight. For the Cosmic Vocation of Man
cannot be fulfilled without making war upon
the causes of Automatic-Subjective-
Compulsion. Thus the Man of Work seeks out
loopholes in this Iron Beast and exploits them
in order that His Message may penetrate
through layer upon layer of deafness and fall
upon the spiritual ears of his brethren, calling
them to arms through sensitivity. Then Man,
himself, will become Virtuous—an
embodiment of the Virtues of Eternity. And
the Virtue of Man shall be his Eternal
Salvation.

Prelude: The Summer of Glory

"They will call this the Summer of Glory. Here, to humble Athar-Ai, will pilgrims flock in droves in years to come. They will have dreams and visions of this place: skies will spit down flecks of amber rain, and set these bloodied battlefields alight. Earth will roar, and open wide its maw; aught that is not pure will be consumed. For when our weapons clash, like cracks of thunder, they will make history. They are the hammer and the anvil of eternity! Can you hear it? Men and women scream for life and death, and every one of them is made eternal. Bodies strewn, boundless, on the plains, sculpted beyond time by love and might. Aye, when your love is pure, your every breath is infinite. Go forth, therefore, my friends, with loving hearts—for those who love you; those who know you not; those who shall, one day, know of your deeds! For we are not men and women, merely... oh, no... we are the authors of a legend. They will call it the Summer of Glory. Step forth if you would join me in its telling."

When Phenelope, who was called by those who loved her 'Sword of Virtue,' ceased to speak, the ground began to quake beneath the furor of a hundred thousand spears. She

did not shrink from the thunderous rapture,
but swelled her breast to meet it, head on.
For but a moment, she felt greater than the
gods, inspired by the worship of her kinsmen.
Yet conscience soon eclipsed her fleeting
pride, and Phenelope was graced by humbler
thoughts- graced indeed, for war was
unbecoming of the citizens of Kath and would
lead only to their downfall if pursued. So
many men and women, who today called
themselves soldiers, were in truth fathers and
mothers, farmers and fishermen, friends and
lovers. Each wore a silver helm upon their
heads, but these sheathes could not conceal
their soft interiors.

Phenelope took pity on them, and
spoke once more: "No, you need not fight for
me!" She stretched her hand across the vale,
and all fell silent. "Who am I? The daughter of
a king? No, I am a lover like you. I will
protect you from what comes. Meanwhile,
return to your homes. I beg you, leave!" The
men who stood before her were perplexed,
each glancing to their neighbour; one or two
broke rank and threw down arms. "Not half a
dozen, of a hundred thousand souls, have
obeyed my command? I said, go home!" No
more soldiers broke their ranks, though many
stood with trembling legs, in indecision.

"Your Grace, we stand beside you til
the end!" exclaimed a man who remained

hidden by his peers. Again and again, voiced by tens of thousands, the infantry cried out, "Til the end! Til the end!"

"So be it," said Phenelope, in whisper. The auroral hour made diamonds of the nervous sweat that beaded on her brow; gilded her ivory skin; wrought of mortal flesh a living goddess. Standing near two metres tall, and flowing with fiery hair, she was as though a sculpture to behold: larger than life, in perfect proportion, a wonder of the natural world whom all adored. Her high-bridged nose and piercing eyes, rumoured to glitter like stars, belied a great compassion for humanity. For she did not confine herself behind her castle walls, but travelled through the townships breaking bread with serfs and noblemen as equals. Indeed, to Athar-Ai had she sojourned as a child, fishing its rivers and tending its herds; kissing shepherds' sons, climbing trees and running barefoot through its fields. Such memories as these would live forever; these summers of glory, untouched by the horrors of war. She, wielding not a sword but a banner; flying the flag of Athar-Ai, which she loved, turned towards the crowning, golden dawn. The echo of impassioned yawps tore quick through the emerald vale, and set the silent grasses to their swaying. That morning, all who fought would fight for her.

The enemy was slow to appear—the legions of Yan-Ora, armour-clad. Each bearing an axe and ebon shield, they numbered as the locusts of the fields. Their minds were bent on bloodshed; each possessed, each driven mad through no fault of their own, but through the turning of the moons and the rhetoric of their tyrant-king. Thus Phenelope felt pity for her foes, knowing surely in her heart that they all had been distorted by forces which could not be controlled. Indeed, this sixth summer of Al-Hrda, by which name is known the first of four 'year-cycles' upon the planet Kath, each determined by its orbit of a different sun, was a time of great turmoil and grief. For the music of its two moons, Tensing and Relasing, had grown discordant on account of a massive roaming comet, called Kismet, which in a bygone age passed so close to Kath that it was scarred by a desert, then collided with the smaller of its moons. This collision caused the moon called Tensing to divert from the orbit it had followed for millions of year-cycles, and to spin in a haphazard way, wobbling and tugging at its planet in constant rebellion. The resulting gravitational disturbance, forever present, yet particularly so during this, the sixth summer of Al-Hrda, caused Kath to lean towards its present sun, making it hellishly hot and altering its people's temperament. So did the rising temperatures awaken, in every man and woman simultaneously, a predisposition towards war.

For nearly two hundred year-cycles, this predisposition had been allayed through the great lunar cultures which existed there, called the Culture of Light and the Culture of Mystery, which had been established at the dawn of civilization by men and women capable of speaking with the stars, who are the ancestors of the arcanists. From time immemorial, the Culture of Light served to venerate and remember the music of the orbit of Relasing, whilst the Culture of Mystery served to venerate and remember the music of the orbit of Tensing. As fate would have it, the orbit of Tensing was greatly altered by the passage of Kismet, whilst Relasing's orbit remained unchanged. Thus the peoples of the Culture of Light, into which Phenelope was born, continued to uphold their traditions, and attempted by creative means to sublimate their lust for war and bloodshed. Meanwhile, the Culture of Mystery was all but lost, and the music of Tensing forgotten, and those nations which had formerly devoted themselves to its practice now permitted the ascendancy of violence. After years of civil conflict, each more tragic than the last, the awakened gods of war sought to manifest a battle between the two cultures of Kath. To this end, there emerged from Yan-Ora a cold-hearted king, called Orthagno, behind whose wealth and power rallied all nations which once practiced the Culture of Mystery.

Desiring to dominate the planet, Orthagno taxed his subjects oppressively and lavished the ill-gotten coin upon architects and arcanists commissioned to build war machines and monsters. After many seasons of preparation, Orthagno's hired armies marched westward, towards the citadel of Il-Sol, which was the stronghold of the Culture of Light. Now Athar-Ai, and the adjacent townships, Hajj-Ai and Fakir-Ai, were all that stood between Orthagno and his prize. Its king, Paragon, had been reluctant to make war upon his brethren from the east, yet the threat of his culture's destruction compelled him to mobilize forces. Paragon, though a wise philosopher, had grown feeble with age and could not lead men into battle. In his stead, his eldest daughter, Phenelope, volunteered to lead with strength and virtue. Though he feared for her safety, the king was reassured by her great competence: having known but ninety seasons upon Kath, Phenelope was prodigious in arcana, architecture and the arts. Therefore, Paragon admitted her request to lead his armies on the condition that she would not, herself, take up arms against Yan-Ora, but merely guide and counsel those who would. Phenelope agreed, and gave her word.

Remembering this sacrosanct promise, and the cosmic trials by which it was foreshadowed; though burning with desire to make war, as did every citizen of Kath, she cried out to the legions of Yan-Ora: "Think upon the families your loyal men and women leave behind. Turn your mind towards death, that you might spare it. Let me fight your champion, Yan-Ora. If, by them, I am slain, my army shall permit your legions pass and claim these humble townships as their own. But if, by me, they are slain, I bid you to return to King Orthagno, and bring to him a gospel of charity. Show to him this scroll, that he might read it and, if his heart is moved, distribute his vast wealth equally to all the people of his kingdoms, including yourselves. I bid you, then, to grow old in the towns of your births, and cross no more into the vale of Athar-Ai. What say you, Yan-Ora? Will you send your champion to me?"

The generals of Yan-Ora convened and, after several minutes of deliberation, instructed the vanguard to part. There emerged from the hoard a gruesome creature bearing the body of a woman, scarred black and bloody with burns. Each mutilation remembered its torture-training at the hands of cruel arcanists, who had poisoned its mind and caused its form to twist into a monster. Its head, from which protruded horns, sat askew upon its torso and swinging from its coccyx was a tail. It snapped like an angry whip, and loosed an ashen scale towards Phenelope, which struck her on the shoulder and drew blood. Its tongue was black, like ash, and forked and flickering. This creature had no name; the reason for its being was war.

The men and women of Athar-Ai had never seen such a creature, and many fled the virgin battlefield. The bowyers took aim at the deserters, ready to fire on Phenelope's word, but she demanded that they lower their arms. Now Yan-Ora's monstrous champion, enraged by her opponent's deep compassion, clasped tight in taloned hands a flaming trident, and aimed it at Phenelope's breast. Yet she, the Sword of Virtue, armed only with a banner, stood fast. "Hear me, abomination," she decreed, then freed the beast's scale from her flesh. The plains fell deathly silent at her gesture. "Your spear may break my body, and your teeth may feast upon my corpse, but I shall rise up, stronger, from the ashes. My blade is wrought of Virtue, fiend. You think it can be broken by your evil?"

The beast snarled, growing bold, and hurled its thrice-fanged weapon at Phenelope. She flexed her broad, powerful back, evading its path and, with hand outstretched, caught the wicked polearm in mid-flight. Spinning it fiercely, like a vortex, before her, its flaming blade began to glow white-hot. The whir of the blade grew loud, and higher in pitch. Meanwhile, all stood silently, in awe. With a sudden start, the burnt beast screamed, and threw itself; its claws; its teeth; its tail towards Phenelope. The whir of the spinning trident was near deafening. All armies cowered low, shielding their ears and crying out, as the beast was consumed by the white-hot blade; swallowed up whole, as though passing through a portal to the Void. The beast was no more, and Phenelope planted her banner. "Go now, sons and daughters of Yan-Ora," she exclaimed. "Tell your king, Orthagno, what you have witnessed. Tell him, also, to disseminate his wealth, and cease to horde the bounties of the land, the sea and sky for the satiation of his bloodlust. Tell him this— tell your king to cease! For, if he does so, every nation shall know peace."

Then the men of Athar-Ai bellowed with joy, and the women shrilly whistled with delight. When the battlefield fell silent once again, the legions of Yan-Ora laid down arms, and prostrated themselves before Phenelope. She walked slowly towards their humbled ranks, with a gait which could inspire song and poetry, and placed into the hands of the lowliest infantryman her scroll, upon which was inscribed her plea to King Orthagno. The infantryman wept as he received it, and swore by life and death to return to Yan-Ora at once, stopping neither for rest nor sustenance until the scroll had been delivered to his king.

On Life after Death

_____

I

It will be like drifting upon a soft current of music and light, which is the eternal quality of the Angels' voices. You give up everything of yourself to this, the magnificent Heaven of Awe, until there is only the music and the light...

You give up everything of yourself until eventually, you have learned the melody and you begin to sing and even contribute your own part. It is at this point that a man is no longer a man, but has become a Free Angel. Now he reunites with his intimates, who are also Free Angels, and creates harmonies and melodies of a sublime nature, whereby the souls of those still sleeping by the sound of this grand lullaby are brought ever-nearer to their Maker. And those who sing have at last crossed the stream, and are delivered into the Sea of Love, for they drift no longer but move at will. And their will is the will of God; their light a gifted light.

A Free Angel is now, as it is his nature to be, only virtue. He is like God, but remains himself. For "Whoever seeks themselves will lose it, but whoever loses themselves for My Sake will have eternal life." Such a man, who is become an Angel, is now infinite; he manifests for the sake of Love, calling all souls into the presence of God, imploring them to die to finitude and to become infinite also.

And those who have been true companions in this life; who have loved and have been loved—whether in consciousness or otherwise—will look for the song of their counterpart in the next. Indeed, they will know it despite appearances, because it will be in perfect harmonization with their own. Therein lies the Beauty of Eternal Reunion, which is the essence of the Heaven of Awe. For all melodies seek their perfect harmony. Were it otherwise, it would cease to be a heaven.

II

The great risk is in clinging to one's personal identity. Clinging to illusions is hell, thus one can abide in a state of hell even as they journey through heaven. Thus heaven and hell are not discrete locations but contrasting states. Heaven is receptivity to the effects of the light; hell is resistance to letting go of what is no longer useful— namely, the personal identity. Hell is a state of continuous threat to one's personal identity—acquired through Automatic Subjective Compulsion—and continuous loss;

it is the friction caused by one's struggling to keep what is destined to be cast aside; indeed, it is the effort to deny Destiny. The state of hell is like that of a jagged stone which the River now carves and polishes. Hell is a state of purgatory—of being purged of one's acquired imbalances. It is the effect of light upon the soul's darkened casing. It is a rude awakening for that soul which has already overslept.

Yet hell is not permanent—for the light will have its way before the end. The rock of evil will be ground to sediment, but the Water of Life will flow into the Sea. All that will remain of you is virtue, and the virtues you manifest in this life shall constitute the entirety of your being in the Eternal Life to come, such that whoever is now rich in virtue will then be rich in substance. Whoever is without virtue in this life has never been born, thus he will not exist in the world to come—for he has not even existed here! The entirety of his presence was constituted by the functioning of Automatic Subjective Compulsion. Yet, if he received but one iota of Warmth in his infancy, or undertook a mite of good in early childhood, he shall exist as such a mite in the hereafter; a tiny flower, cherished by sensitive souls.

For whatever are one's virtues are one's being—for all beings are, in their essential nature, only virtue. Whatever is not virtuous is not, and whatever is virtuous is eternal. But what is virtue? It is the capacity, whether consciously or otherwise, to submit to the influence of the Higher Intelligences; to bow before one's God and His attendants. It is from such a state of faithful submission that all virtuous conduct proceeds. Yet one may only, in this life, consciously submit to the light in the presence of darkness. Indeed, it is the freedom to choose between light and darkness that permits conscious submission—choice being the product of one's freedom. Thus one is capable of conscious virtue who is free, and he is free who is first tempted. For the Higher Intelligences and Lower Intelligences were created by a single Thought, and manifest for a single purpose.

There is, moreover, the virtue of Innocence, which proceeds spontaneously from the creatures of the Animal Kingdom, and all of Plant Life also. For beings such as these manifest themselves in complete accordance with the will of their Creator, but do so unconsciously, without knowledge. Theirs is one portion of heaven: the Heaven of Home, which is called the Garden of Eden. Yet the consciousness of Man was cast from the garden on account of his freedom—and consequent forgetfulness of Innocence—such that he must now work to regain what he has lost, in order that he might regain it sevenfold. For Man was once an infant, and was Innocent; that infant-soul exists even now within the Garden of Eden and, if he listens well to its cries, it will be his guide back to the Heaven of Home. Thus all men and women of maturity are implored to remember their Innocence—and go to it. For the memory of Innocence is the foundation upon which every conscious Virtue is established.

The Cloister

———————

I stole an apple from the lips of Eve;
A thorn from raging lion's paw I rent—
She humbly thankéd me,
Then ventured to present
The means through which
All wrongs are righted;
Earth shall dance again,
And be delighted!

"Instinct cloistered in concepts
Of Truth and Beauty, fair of face,
Wherein undying Love awaits."

Aglow with heav'nly harmony,
Transfigured and illumined, she
Revealed to me her Truthful form
That tragic hours may be reborn
Into a world where innocence abounds:
Sweet Mary, e'er a virgin, round
With child, who, in this sanctuary,
Prays upon the coming of her Lord.

And the Lord shall come to her,
For she has prayed.

The Voice of Love

The Natural Imagination is a stopping point, not a destination. "For Love has spoken on the coming Spring, and stolen off with Winter's deathly sting!" Through its Revelatory Prism, Love speaks, revealing Destiny: eternal life! Having heard, one must now make headway towards the manifestation of Destiny. Speech for speaking's sake is not enough; hearing for hearing's sake is not enough. Now one must cut away all that is not life; all manifestations of the great beast, Automatic Subjective Compulsion, and hold fast to all that is living. One must concentrate one's Thoughts exclusively upon life, doing away with all nebulous and peripheral mentation. Neither the pursuit of pleasure, nor the aversion of pain, should stand in the way of this holy quest. One's Love must remain strong—or, one must remain vulnerable enough to receive Love into one's being. For Love says to all of us: "You shall not die, I shan't let you!"

Now all Men and Women of Conscience work together as vicegerents of Love, each supporting the other in their time of flagging, such that no soul now destined for life should perish on its way. Let those who fall be lifted up, as strength is married with compassion, and none who know true Love shall ever perish. Thus the work of the lover is to lift up his flagging brethren and usher them towards their ultimate Destiny, the Most-Holy Sunset. In order that one be made capable of doing so, he must first know the likeness of that Destiny, and it is made known by the voice of Love, which is made manifest through the prismatic emanations of the Natural Imagination. Therefore, the Work begins with the opening of the Natural Imagination, but does not thereafter end. Yet what lies beyond this work cannot be written.

For now unfolds the spiritual vocation of mankind as it is: the submission to Love's instruction for the reunion of one's God within Oneself. "And He told them this parable, that they should find strength within themselves to pray and not to faint."

Love and Kindness

———————————

What is a worthy theme but Love,
Which is each day and hour renewing?
And lovers who are true, and so eschewing
Gross mortality? Love holds fast. It moves
Not with the mountains, when they quake,
But lowly bends for tender flowers
Strewn careless o'er the Fields of Fate.
Love is kind. It dances on the breeze;
It offers signs to lovers who would
Nurture its new-planted seeds. For,
Ever there is kindness, there is love,
As where there swells a verdant bud
A blossom shall emerge, by Nature's grace,
Love from kindness blooms apace, apace!

For the Harvester (II)

Are we not star-fire?
Are we not golden,
Bold, exploding supernovae,
Echoed 'neath a loving mortal gaze?
Envisioning your soul, your sacral face
Some light-years yonder, cloaked in wondrous
Nebulae, I, dreaming or remembering,
Inquire: are we not, too, in distant space,
Two fulgent stars, two galaxies?
Are we, by mass and gravity,
Not caused to falter and to sway
From orbiting majestically and harkening
The blissful-silent music of the spheres?
Yet as I flow towards you, dear,
I grow towards the sun and I am smitten!
Swimming weightlessly as water,
Or as mercury runs silvern through
The fingers of the morn;
Effortless, I soar on gilded wings
About your lissom form...
All time, all temporality,
Adjoins with cosmic sovereignty,
For by your touch, I cease;
Here, in your arms, I vanish to myself...

And yet I am,
And we're as tandem deities—together!
Newborn wishing-stars for now and ever...

(Or mayhap tigers!—elder sphinxes,
Which or both I cannot say)
We are the free; divine and blissful
As we kiss, and set our course
As if two travelers in the wistful
Desert, gasping towards such bright,
Cool, cleansing wellsprings which we are,
Wherein, corporeally, I perish;
Wherein my spirit rises,
Whirls about you as a dancing dervish...
For you, my sweet oasis, are splendid!—
Twice-beautiful in every known respect;
Thrice-so in each unknown as yet!
Refreshing,
Life-giving
Serendipity,
Ecstatic
On my trembling tongue a joy, a jewel;
A rare and precious morsel for the soul.
Henceforth shall I prize you and protect you;
Keep you close till Time and come-what-may
Shall our two yearning spirits make as One.

You are the dawn, my love:
Harvester of my heart,
Author of the coming diamond days.

Diogenes' Dream

OF GENESIS, APOCALYPSE &
THE PURSUIT OF PLEASURE

A LYRICAL DRAMA OF TWO ACTS

DRAMATIS PERSONAE

DEITIES
DIANA, the queen of heaven
    (and the DOE)
VOLUPTAS, the maiden goddess
    (and the LOVEBIRD)
HEPHAESTUS, lord of violence
    (and the BOAR)
SIRIUS, gatekeeper of life and death
    (and the BITCH)

ALSO,
FURIES
ANGLERFISH

MORTALS
DIOGENES, the first philosopher
SAPPHO, tenth muse of mortal birth

ALSO,
POETS
MEN
CHORUS, the audience in attendance

ACT I, SCENE I

The darkest hour of night looms over Athens.
Diogenes sleeps soundly in a cavern when the
first ray of an Augustine dawn — Diana,
Queen of Heaven —transforms into a doe and
goes to him.

Chorus: Amidst the glare, we turned to look:
We saw a doe, so fleet afoot;
She, dancing in the August air,
Was subject to the earnest stare
Of our dark eyes; in her we saw
A deity! Thus, overawed and glad,
We half-recalled an ancient tale
Which humankind has oft regaled,
For now we see, as plainest fact:
The Gods of Old remain intact!
Though cynics scoff and disbelieve,
The gods shall rule eternally!
So have we now, face to face,
Perceived beyond the commonplace,
For cooing doves portend the play
Of fair Diana Cervidae.
Pray, Diana, please impart
To us the drama in your heart
Which e'en the animals descry;
Which sings the Truth, the Way, the Life;
Wherein the light of Love shines, everlasting!

Diana: If truth is your desire, I shall speak it:
Few indeed are those who truly seek it.

This is as much the beginning of Time,
As the dawning of a millenary age;
A trifling hope, a trinket
 Of we gods who shape its days
And grant noble philosophers
To glimpse, then long to ponder
O'er the providence of Love's mysterious ways.
For soon shall star-eyed angels near
The Earth, full-gowned and veiled
In russet flesh, to found a kingdom
Of a thousand years' regale;
A thousand springs, a thousand summers—
Ever after, golden slumbers
In Elysium, upon the rolling dales!
Thus Sirius, of sound yet quaint
Proclivity, has taken on the likeness
Of a bitch and lain beside Diogenes,
Unseen within his cavern's lightless
Niche, in hope that he might fathom of
That perfect, glad millennium—and pray,
Not to be blinded by its brightness....

> *The shimmering portent star, Sirius, descends
> from the heavens disguised as a common
> bitch. She, too, is drawn to Diogenes. He stirs,
> and appears to awaken.*

Diogenes: What shines before Aurora
Rises, tender and amaranthine,
Portending cruel Egyptian summers;
Crowned by an aureole of canine
Aspect? Wake, ye doves, go sound a warning—

Fly this dazzling, dogged morning!
Wake, ye doves, too gentle and benign!
For this, the hour of my glory,
Nears to me in plain disguise—
What fool shall e'er believe my story?
Better I should run and hide
Lest she, whom Hindus call Kali,
Should drain the blood of life from me
And leave my body buried in the soil!
Lest by her bite I be awakened,
From my cavern I must hasten—
For, in truth, this bitch is Death
To me; and from my lungs, bereft
Of wind, shall draw forth words
Of praise. Yet I, enchanted; lured
Towards her lolled and blackened tongue
Shall raise my eyes, with love ablaze,
To Sirius, the shining one; the dog-star!

> *Diogenes prostrates, trembling before the bitch, Sirius. As he does so, she reveals her true form: that of a beautiful, dark-skinned goddess of the sky with eyes aglow like star-fire.*

Sirius: What's this you speak of? What is …
'love?' I have not heard this word before.

Diogenes: It is the taste of cool ambrosia;
The wings that cause me soar
On blissful winds to breathe th'aroma
Of infinitude and awe.

Sirius: Forsooth, I take you 'neath my wing—
We journey to a sacred spring
Of love beyond Olympus' highest heights.
So please, speak not of tastes and smells
Which your five mortal senses have beheld:
My scythe shall rend them from thine spirit's eye,
That it might gaze more clearly at the skies....

> *Sirius brings forth a silver scythe and prepares*
> *to take Diogenes' life. Upon the moment of*
> *truth, however, she drops her blade and points*
> *towards a portent in the sky....*

Yet here now shines an omen
From above—a rarest moon!
'Neath which heav'nly lumen
Such as I are coarsely hewn
Into bodies more becoming of
The pigeon and the mourning dove:
Herein, I can but fall for thee,
My simple, sweet Diogenes,
Whom I shall love until the end of days.

Diogenes: A lunatic am I;
The song of spring upon my ears!

Sirius: Yet still I must away, for tragic times
Are drawing, by the moment, nearer!

Diogenes: Tragic times ... wait! Shall you return?

231

Sirius: I shall—upon th'apocalypse,
Ordained by morning's star—
Meanwhile, beneath the tardy moon,
Voluptas and the lyric bard of Lesbos
Shall unfold their tragic yarn to list'ning ears.

> *Sirius kisses Diogenes on the forehead before transforming back into a bitch and dashing away. Diana Cervidae approaches in her stead. She is followed by Hephaestus and Voluptas who, to mortal eyes, possess the bodies of a boar and lovebird. These three uncommon creatures of the wood approach Diogenes, yet he sees them not, and remains wholly enamoured by the bitch.*

Diogenes: So soon, my love?
You vanish through the trees ...
Still, your ling'ring whisper,
Speaking to my soul, foresees
The authorship and ruin of the ages:
A book of flowered words and gilded pages;
Prophecies attended by astrologers and sages,
Writ anew with every passing season
On all Hearts of Love and Minds of Reason.

> *Diana licks Diogenes playfully on the earlobe. He falls instantly unconscious, as though asleep within a dream. Now Diana, with the aid of her companions, spirits his body into the abode of the gods.*

ACT I, SCENE II

In this far, celestial realm, the true forms of the gods are revealed: Diana is resplendent, cloaked with golden wings; Voluptas is more beautiful than life; Hephaestus' eyes, dark as coal-fire, stir with guileful schemes and machinations.

Diana: 'Twas a lonely, distant darkness
Which the mind of Chaos wrought
Upon our hopeful heaven; godless
Were the nights he brought
Beyond the hallowed halls of Nyx
And Hypnos. His derisive trick
Was made unmanifest by Love,
Whose clear, lucid light illumed
The very wick; the hearth-fire of
The universe—the eye beholding starlight.
Thus, as lovely lyrics are to rhyme,
Our Love would come to know us
Though the hearts of humankind,
Who beseeched the stars, in chorus,
Grace to seek, and grace to find.
Therefore, Man—too nebulous;
Whose eyes, naive and credulous,
Peer ignorant into our holy night—
Was destined to shine iridescent;
Brighter than the lunar crescent,
Truly, to all Nocturne a delight.
For in each pupil he containéd

Every constellation painted
In this arc of heav'n—it's every Joy!
And that he might one day cognize
Their brilliance, I, with knowing mind,
Drew back upon my bowstring and
Employed Hephaestus, Lord of Flame,
To immolate a single, dark-bane
Arrow of my longing. Thus, I might
Imprint upon his soul a hungry vision;
Slit through milky skin, a fine incision
Through which spirit-seeds might dip and rise,
At once towards the Earth and t'wards the Skies.
Now all we gods longed for the day
Their germination might allay
The woes of distant galaxies and stars.
And though Man was still but a seed,
Hephaestus laboured; hammered, heaved
To cause his mortal shell to break
And bring forth everlasting leaves
When, at last, within his forge,
Where hammers crash and fires roar,
Our Smith's unyielding alchemy
Fermented Man's sweet effigy—
Yet corked it with his furor and haste.
This curse was like a thorny rose;
This boon a wolf in woollen robes,
Yet had been, by Our Cosmos, preordained.

> *In his attempts to shape the body of humanity,*
> *lame Hephaestus blinds Diogenes with fire;*
> *strikes him with his cane and breaks his leg.*
> *As Diogenes howls with pain, Voluptas gently*
> *takes him in her arms….*

Nonetheless, Voluptas sought
Naively, with o'erweening heart,
To spare Man's mortal suffering
And wake him with a comforting
Embrace, that he might swell
With amber fruits and asphodels.
For she believed her brother
But a boar, and I a doe;
And ardently did seek another
Way to wake Man's soul.
Alas—the youngest deity of heaven,
Too child-like to foresee our veiled intentions!
Thus, Pleasure sought her brother and inquired:

Voluptas: What might it take to soothe
This Man of Sorrow;
Rouse him from his slumber
And enliven him by 'morrow's
Gentle morn? Behold, his sleep unsound;
His thoughts beyond those vital bounds
Which are becoming of a man of flesh and blood;
Who calls himself 'philosopher,' yet is a beast
In Truth: his angel dreams and, dreaming, sleeps;
He, animated yet deceased to my fair charms;
A cosmic paradox, unconscious in my arms….

Hephaestus: Greed, lust, fearfulness and ego
Have blinded him to all things right and regal;
Bear witness to these frightful mechanisms,
Which shall bring about his spirit's schism:

With hunger he sickens,
Yet thinks it a boon;
This ailment, contagious,
Strikes morning and noon.
By moonlight he kindles
The sexual fires;
Their sweetness, dissembled,
A product of ire.
He fearfully weaves
Through the graves
Of the dead—
He thinks them alive
But is gravely misled!
He rots in the ground,
Yet he proudly decrees:
"Behold: I am healthy
And free from disease!"

Diana: Aghast, Voluptas beckoned him:

Voluptas: Will he not wake for knowledge?
The scrolls of ancient augurs—
Will he reckon and acknowledge them?
 For Arts and Fair Creations—
Will not Man for these awaken?
Nay? Then I shall give myself—
Crown of Heaven's bounteous wealth—
In marriage to him that he might arise!

Diana: Then, even as Voluptas spake,
Diogenes began to wake!
His eyes grew wide as he beheld
Her beauty; how his bosom swelled!
Such that Hephaestus came to fear
His precious sister might endear
This son of mortal men more than him.

Hephaestus: Voluptas, my pet,
Your motives are pure,
Yet Man shall not venture
To drink down your cures.
Nay, none of your virtues
Shall move him from here—
Only ego, greed, lust and fear!

> *At Hephaestus' command, Diogenes' wonder
> abates. In its stead arises lust, which causes
> him to masturbate and roughly grasp Voluptas
> by the breast. She shrieks and recoils.*

Voluptas: Alack! Half-built, unseemly,
Have you shaped my groom to be!
I scarcely know his likeness
From the demons of Hades!

Hephaestus: Indeed—
This man is blind to you;
He shall, a violent roué,
Rend your consecrated clothes;
Sting you like a serpent

Slinking through the undergrowth;
In waking shall defile you with
His vile, corrupted ways,
Yet, dreaming, shall remain
Your mild and ever-loyal slave....

Diana: Yet Pleasure, like Parmenides,
Thought long upon the Truth
And offered Man indemnity
In place of just reproof:

Voluptas: I grant him friendship
In the face of every ill,
And though he loves me not,
I love him still.

Hephaestus: Love ... sweet love ...
It shall pass, and you shall see
That naught within your power
Shall awake humanity.
And so, for fear my kindly, decent
Kin might suffer needlessly,
I swear to grant four seasons
To the Earth, which has too frequently
Distracted your enchanting gaze
From my grotesquely blemished face.
Therefore, when spring and summer,
Followed by autumnal breeze,
Give way to bleak mid-winter,
Life and love shall wither 'neath
My will; Voluptas, you'll be free
To abrogate the wedding-vow you've taken—
For I shall turn the tide on foul 'humanity'

And drive it to the grave, or else insanity.

Voluptas: No! Please, I beg you!

Hephaestus: That you might take my hand
And with your brother make amends....

Voluptas: Never!

> *Now Sirius, enrobed in light once more, returns
> to the abode of the gods—and is horrified by
> what has come to pass....*

Sirius: Voluptas, please—do hear me out
Lest you be driven mad, or worse!
And curse the moment of your birth—
For you shall never win the heart
Of him for whom all bitches bark:
'Twas in the wood, upon the morn,
That I revealed my heavn'ly form
To him and swore to love him—hark
My words—until the rapture!
Thus I bid you, sacral kin,
Your wedding vow to Man rescind:
Speak neither 'evermore' nor 'ever after.'

Voluptas: Wed whom, I pray, in place of him?
Sing what in place of lovesick hymns?
For whilst I cannot sing or speak,
My wedding vow I can still keep—
I'll keep it evermore and ever after—
Though it cause my gentle soul to fracture!

Diana: With these words, the Friend of Man
Rent off her graceful silken gowns;
Hastened t'wards the coastal sands
And threw her body to the ground,
Forever to lament her tragic fate.

Hephaestus: Voluptas, wait!

> *She does not look back. Aggrieved,
> Hephaestus cries out and strikes Diogenes
> with vengeful fury.*

Sirius: How dare you lord your violent will
Over humankind! Cause Earth no ill
Lest Heaven meet its own untimely end!
Surely you must know this, sacral friend?

Hephaestus: You deal men death
But shudder when they cry?
Then death I give to them—
And absolutely naught besides!

> *True to his word, Hephaestus wrests Sirius'
> scythe from her and places it—together the
> right to take life—into mortal hands.*

Diana: So Hephaestus placed a scythe
Into the hands of humankind.
Yet think upon his sister—wist!
Whose love for mortals would persist
Though every sibling, son and daughter,
Cast in consternation; slaughtered

By her brother's cruel, incestuous wish!
Yet as Hephaestus sought to end
Voluptas' love for mortal Men,
I, with pity in my heart,
Exhaled a sigh, alike the lark,
And brought forth from my breast
A righteous Woman. Too, for fear she
Linger near the planets and the stars,
I lit an earthly fire; placed desire in her heart
And named her aft' the colour of my tears,
Falling sapphire as the Medit'ranean mere.

> *Sappho, tenth muse of mortal birth, bathes in*
> *unsettled seas while dreaming of a lover yet*
> *unknown....*

Though the heavens knew it not,
My Sappho, like a sea-bird, sought
To auger crashing waves and beheld
Voluptas' cry of love, cast into Hell:

Voluptas: O, Earth! I never wished to be
A demon or a scourge:
I sought but to love you
Till the end of days—upon my word!
Ne'er did I desire that end
To come; to be its savage source:
Merely to inspire you, friend,
And speed you on your heav'nly course.
Though, by my brother's wicked will
Four seasons shall too swiftly pass,
Then on the winter—hear me well—
All mortal Men shall be dispatched

Into the underworld to meet their doom,
And I to insanity and everlasting gloom!

> *As Voluptas' sobs of grief echo in the winds
> and rains; in all that manifests, and all that lies
> still hidden, Sappho comprehends the fate of
> all....*

ACT I, SCENE III

> *Voluptas sits, distraught, upon a cold and
> lonely beach.   Diana Cervidae surveys its
> shores.*

Diana: Spring ... summer ... autumn's leaf-fall
All gave way to winter.
The whole of Pleasure's agony
Was spent upon a scream—
For frost now gripped the Earth
Whereon she'd waited hopefully.

> *Voluptas screams with grief! At her command,
> the skies grow darkly ominous.   Men and
> women leave their homes, seeking out the
> source of heaven's cry.   Even the stars and
> planets grow concerned...*

Sirius: Pray, Hephaestus, ease her pain—
And from mankind's destruction
I beseech you to refrain,
For in mortal hearts there are

Unnumbered worlds, uncounted stars.
Take heed of this injunction
To forego my grisly function—
For, should a single soul
Be deconstructed without care,
Even we in heav'n shall be
Corrupted and despair!

Hephaestus: I'll not be the death of Man—
'Tis by his own ignoble hand
That Armageddon shall occur,
Himself the only murderer!
For you have merely reaped the ripe,
And I have merely giv'n them strife—
Yet none so great that they cannot endure.
'Tis Ignorance, the closest friend
Of this collusive company,
Through which attempts to make amends
All come to cruel, untimely ends;
Which causes boastful rivalry
And rends them into factions.
Look! See how they gather
To dispute the will of God;
Vying lords of mind and matter
Rule them with their iron rods—
Violence spreads like fire in the wind!

Sirius: Though your argument rings true,
I cannot help but weep and rue
For those who'll die upon the beach,
My scythe already swung for me.
For Man shall harvest of itself;
Corrupt our holy commonwealth.

So I'll take my leave of here to warn
A friend of coming woes; I swore
To treat him faithfully:
Diogenes of Sinope.

> *Sirius descends from the heavens, seeking her lover.   Hephaestus, meanwhile, spreads dissent and sows the seeds of war…*

Diana: Now Fury murmured 'neath
A jealous ocean wrought of tears,
Made salty by the weeping
Of a thousand martyred seers.
Whilst the weak and self-fulfilling
Shrunk away from death therein,
The strong, the brave and willing,
Argued that to flee was sin;
Though the former would survive
The brutal trials which were to come,
The latter were the more alive
E'en as their flesh succumbed
To drowning darkness.

ACT I, SCENE IV

> *In a vast emerald forest, filled with fey and mystery, the Poets of Ancient Greece sing and converse.   Shade trees, full with leaves, obscure their vision of the growling sky…*

Diana: Nearby, a band of poet-seers
Had gathered in the wood

To lounge among we smiling deer
Who took our fibrous food,
With Hesiod and Homer at the fore.
Each man and women sang
Their tune; each heart the larger
For it. But a single song rang
True, voiced by a mythic martyr:
She, a blue-eyed poetess,
Called Sappho of the Sable Rock,
Stood to offer her address
To hearts enrapt and glad
Upon a solemn vision she'd had.

> *Sappho stands to address her fellows; they
> listen with careful attention ...*

Sappho: Once, rambling through the forest
In which Pan sought sinless Syrinx,
I saw an agéd oak with knotted roots.
Thereunder, I reclined to drink
A quickened mead of sleep beside a brook.
As I slumbered, nestled in its boughs,
I dreamt I saw a doe, with glory crowned.

> *Diana Cervidae approaches Sappho...*

How she, so graceful, feminine,
With starlight on her back,
Elaborated on the ancient tales;
A straightened arrow fired
From Diana's mystic bow,
Sent to end these days of violence!
The coo of doves assuaged her steps;

The cherry lovebirds pipped
A wild remembrance freshly writ,
Like tinder to my candle's wick.

Diana: These dark times, these trials:
Do not forsake them!
Rise and seize your rightful
Place beyond these warring heavens.
See with thine own spirit's eye
The star Love has ordained
To marry with your presence:
Grant an earnest serenade
To her, that you might lessen
The burdens which her love
For you have brought.
Thus I present a songbook
Which was wrought in secret
At the Dawn of Time, known
To neither mortal nor god,
Containing salubrious rhyme:
Written on its pages is the key
To awakening remembrance
Of the Beautiful and Free.
When the winds rush cold
And the lamps burn dark,
Light shall yet shine therein;
When the stars enfold,
Their treasures locked
Behind the fears of men,
Sing its verse—that love might live again!

Diana vanishes and the air grows eerily silent. The leafy canopy recedes, and the angry sky beyond comes into view. Poets shudder at the sight of it, yet through it know that Sappho speaks the truth.

ACT I, SCENE V

Having heard the prophecy of Sappho, the Poets of Ancient Greece leave the forest and accompany her to the beach. With songbook in hand, she seeks true love. Diana Cervidae walks amongst them.

Diana: Water's quick to boil;
The hottest tidal currents flow
Where Gretchen, oyster goddess,
Transforms poesy into pearl.
Thus, all just and modest
Men abiding in the wood
Accompanied their prophet
To the sea, whose changing mood
Was subject of the saddest
Songs; most furious and gladdest
Songs that ever have been
Sung by sons of men.
Yet tongues attuned to melody
Have frequent cause to rest;
Beside a cavern, breathlessly,
They stopped for wine and bread
But recoiled from scraping footsteps

Drawing near.

Diogenes, blinded and crippled by the gods,
emerges from the darkness of his cavern.

Then emerged Diogenes
From deep within his darkened cave;
Heir to every foulness, he
Abhorred the inauspicious days
We gods wrought o'er the Earth,
Groaning with misery and dearth.
Blazing-eyed, he swore to slay
All men who dared trespass
Too near the entrance to his cave.
All but Sappho fled him, fearing
Deathly tolls or disappearing,
Ne'er again to see the light of day.
Sappho boldly struck his face
And then exclaimed aloud:

Sappho: Diogenes the Cynic, stand down!

Diogenes: Stand down, you say—
On what account?
Your army is a farce;
You wield neither weaponry
Nor dark, infernal arts!

Diana: The Cynic laughed hysterically
As Sappho slapped him once again
And spoke to him of Truth:

Sappho: I revere what you profane;

Your threats are void and moot;
Wrath shall not drive me away,
For I have travelled far—
And travel farther still,
To court a distant star.

Diana: Diogenes then wretched and spat:

Diogenes: Speak not of stars to me!
I knew a heav'nly lover, once:
She vanished through the trees,
And nary shall we meet again
Till flames hail from the sky
To spite the foolish whim of Man,
Which scorched the Earth with eyes
Too dark to see the future; hands
Too clumsy to design a better way.
No pale, mortal woman can allay
The pain I feel; for love is lost
To me, this precious bounty
Of the soul is turned to dust
And buried in the ground.
Behold—I am the crownéd
Heir of darkness!

Sappho: Then may you dig, Diogenes,
And show us where it hides!
With spades of living metaphor
We shall unearth your occult bride
And restore her to her rightful groom.

Diana: Diogenes then laughed and wept
To hear those Sapphic words;

As Beauty touched his sickly heart,
A love long-sleeping stirred
And caused his blackened soul's illumination.

> *Sappho helps Diogenes to his feet and comforts him.*

The Cynic spoke nostalgically
And offered up his song;
Thereafter, lilting poets' feet
He guided and made strong
Due to his many seasons in the wilds.
Towards the beach he led them
Just as quickly as could be;
Kept company with Sappho;
Whispered faint and eerily
His tale of star-crossed love into her ear:

> *As the entourage makes haste towards the sea, Diogenes and Sappho trail behind in private conversation...*

Diogenes: Have you seen my Trackless Vestal,
Disappeared without a trace?
She makes conversation with the echoes;
Calls the blades of tender grass by name ...
Too, the blades of men, stained lifeless red.
You dally where she lies, where she lingers,
Where she lives ... in the graves ...
In the February primrose.

Sirius draws near, having sought Diogenes for many days. Sappho sees her and exclaims with surprise:

Sappho: Oh! Your Vestal goes a-roaming
Through the wood today—
A tragic tale comes rolling
Off your tongue, before the spring!

Diogenes: Sirius, my love!

Sirius: Spring indeed—
Though winter's deathly
Sting must firstly come.
As darkest Night precedes
The Morn, a father to the sun,
I greet you in the flesh
And fervently forewarn
You of inevitable Death;
A sounding horn am I,
Whose dulcet tenor tells
Of yonder beach Hephaestus
Has transformed into a Hell!

Diogenes: No, breathe into me once
Before my death: I shall outlive
Dark fires and grim catastrophes,
And torrents and endure to give
My love to you, O gentle breeze!
So be a kind and clement thief:
Pluck out my blinded eyes,
That I might come to know and see
Your haunting beauty with my mind

And with fervent imaginings aspire
Towards the star of Sirius,
To be your mortal squire!

Sirius: Know that I have held a place
In store for such a man as you.
With vision of idyllic charm and grace
Thou shalt eschew all heinous things
And follow Sappho, whose broad wings
Shall course you through the gates
Of Our Unending Lord's Elysium!

> *By Sirius' touch, Diogenes' ailments are transferred to her. The grim wretch is restored to his true form, that of a noble philosopher, whilst Sirius becomes crippled and decrepit.*

Until that hour we meet again,
I shall conceal your lust and sin
Within a sea whose anglerfishes
Swallow souls who have no wishes
To cognize we cosmic mysteries;
To greet immortal deities
And long-forgotten kings.

> *Hephaestus harkens from the heavens, meanwhile, and overhears the oath which Sappho speaks...*

Sappho: I shall see him through alive,
Upon my life and honour.
Failing this, I'll keenly strive

To sing a song so sonorous
That heaven shall be purified by tears.

> *Sirius vanishes, seeming contented in spite of
> her pain. At last, the Poets emerge from the
> wood and set foot on the beach.*

ACT I, SCENE VI

Hephaestus: That band of poets has arrived
Upon my deadly shores;
The brutish and the beautiful
Are both aptly accounted for:
Sweet Sappho and the sour Diogenes.
The twain, too near awakening,
Whose zeal to win the Truth
I seek to break; to wean my sister
From her youthful fancies,
I shall bear the chalice of dissent....

> *Hephaestus approaches Voluptas, who sits
> distraught upon the barren beach. He offers
> her a drink to 'comfort' her...*

Voluptas: What ... what's this?

Hephaestus: It's naught but tonic,
From which clarity shall ensue.

Voluptas: The smell is offish ...
As though with sorcery imbued—
I will not drink!

Hephaestus: Why must you question me?
I am your brother...

> *Voluptas takes the chalice and drinks reluctantly. After a moment, she gasps, as if stricken by poison, and falls to her knees, enraged!*

Could I, to childish reason,
Hope to show that love and war
Are like in nature: deathly demons,
Clad in skin of rotting sores?
Both are as a wave of trembling-terror...

> *Voluptas slowly stands, then shrieks and throws the chalice to the ground, turning her maddened gaze towards the mortals! She calls upon the Furies, who respond to the whims of her wrath...*

Sappho: That wave!—unbridled feral force
Conducted by the Furies
Who whip the raging waters,
Riding rapidly and surely
On the maddened devil-horse
The Lord Hephaestus conjures forth!

Hephaestus: The troubled and the weary,
Fallen on my sandy shores,
Heaved lungs of salted water;
Marked by Death, they wore

His shroud upon their fragile souls.
Whilst curs and cowards fled away,
The brave and righteous still remained;
They sought to soothe my sister,
Whom mankind has made insane—
Her love for them, by witchcraft, stayed!

Sappho: Pray my song, the Song of Seasons,
Might sound out above this storm:
May all Men awake to Reason;
Pleasure's beauty be reborn
Through a single, solemn poetess!

> *Sappho scrambles for her songbook, humming
> an enchanted tune. Voluptas' rage passes
> and the Furies stand down as she does so.
> She stops Sappho and puts her book aside.*

Voluptas: I blush ...
For I adore you though I know you not,
And court you with a coy familiarity;
Lapsed, as though a dark night's dream,
Your face alone could speak a lover's memory...

Hephaestus: What Power has defied my will—
Which stars stand undivided?
My own sister, mad and blinded,
How could you love this mortal more than me?
Why, I'll rend the heav'n and earth asunder!—
Strike, alike a serpent's fang;
Naught but flesh shall sate my hunger!
Cease your struggle, callow mustang—

I shall have the comp'ny of your soul!

> *Hephaestus grabs Sappho and drags her away; Sappho fights against him to no avail. Voluptas' madness returns and the Furies attack!*

Diogenes: Now the raging hurricane
Bears both fair and wretched things
Away; fierce gales and driving rains
Uproot the ancient totem trees
And rend a level plane the Earth and Heav'n.

> *Diogenes and Furies fight to the death upon the cacophonous shore, while breakers crash and thunder cracks around them...*

O Sirius, I pray thee,
Grant me strength!—for naught shall save me
From the steely grip of Death, O balmy Death!

> *Diogenes is slain and consumed by the sea...*

ACT II, SCENE I

> *Nothing is seen. Only darkness, wherein voices softly speak...*

Hephaestus: Do you reckon where you are?

Sappho: I see nothing... nothing... nothing.

Hephaestus: Behold ye your beloved star?

Sappho: Nothing... nothing... nothing.

Hephaestus: Yet it is everywhere,
And therefore something.
It fills my savage soul, an ichor pumping
Through my veins, causing Nature's Holy Law
To diminish and decay. Before the birth of Love,
It ruled the skies: naught but fools and children
Dare conceive it otherwise; a fairy-story by which
Infants colour moths and maggots as resplendent
Butterflies. All was born of Void, love included—
Look no further for the truth, or you'll
Forever be deluded by the fantasies of sickly
Lesser beings who've neither ears for hearing,
Eyes for seeing. The Apocalypse has come
And all shall meet its stony gaze before their end!
Neither night nor day, nor bitter enemy nor friend
Shall endure this blight sound and unshriven.

Sappho: Should we not at least attempt
To manifest our God-given
Qualities, fair or foul,
As the fact—the very fact—
Of our existence would allow?

Hephaestus: Life is truly godless without Love,
Which mortal men have stolen from
We very stars above!

Sappho: You question your existence in this Void?

This place of your creation, by which every
Human nation has been robbed of aught
It loves; of every trace of Hope and Joy?
So you are a fool, for you are Death,
And death is real. Hear my song, its zeal,
And pray, repent! Right this cosmic wrong
Which heav'n and earth rightly resent!

Hephaestus: You foolish little child,
Think ye a chanted dirge or elegy
Shall stay me from this path
Of self-destruction? It shall not!
Each mortal soul who sought
To take Voluptas for themselves
Shall know immortal wrath
Before the final, deathly knell!
For my sister, who is dead to me;
Too like a fallen apple, she loved
Your kin too keenly to be dutiful.
The moment she set eyes on you,
My spirit drowned in hateful lies—
What good, I ask, is singing now?
Your tuneless, acid lullabies
Have made her fall from heav'n
And lose her innocence of mind!
So I seek my vengeance:
Meet your enemy, Hephaestus!
You assault upon the senses
Of the gods; my sister's weakness!

Hephaestus' burning hate lights up the void, revealing churning magma fonts which swallow the bones of the dead and the dreams of the jaded. He takes Sappho by the hair, and goes to feed her to eternal, hungry fires...

Sappho: I pray you, Lord of Violence,
You know not what you seek:
Your poet shall be silenced,
Trodden clay beneath your feet!

The cruel god's pride is piqued. He lets her go and hears what she would say...

Hephaestus: None e'er dared to praise me,
Darkened Star.

Sappho: For none know how vile you are.
How could any know your mind?

Hephaestus: My guile is legendary!

Sappho: Yet your scheming's too unkind
To win the praise of missionaries.
I, however, am a poetess
And shall, for heaven's sake,
Proffer you my hope, my love,
My everlasting faith!

Sappho bows before Hephaestus. He stands down, powerless to cause her harm, yet schemes to bring about her death and downfall.

Hephaestus: Then prove yourself, my little slave:
Bring Voluptas back to me.
Seek her in th'infernal womb
Of Hell, where demons loom;
Where Sirius weeps o'er the grave
Of her belovéd mortal groom.
Yet silently I bid you go about
Those poison-fumes and gouts
Of steam. Should Sapphic song
Befall her ears, or dare ye to be seen,
You shall be reckoned meek and mean;
Falsely accused of eschewing the oath
You swore to her and her betrothed:
Diogenes was swallowed by the mere
'As you fled him, overcome by fear.'

Sappho: 'Struth, you wear the devil's clothes:
By you I was beaten, dragged away!
Were it otherwise, I would have stayed
Until the wild winds carried me to sea,
Contented to have perished like a rose
Whose buried bulb shall blossom in the spring.

Hephaestus: Your rosebud
Shall be full and flowering
To suit my ends; so to the depths of Hell
Your gallant soul I now commend.

> Hephaestus points the way to Hell. Sappho solemnly obeys.

ACT II, SCENE II

> *Several Anglerfish hover eerily still and statuesque about the deep, volcanic rock of Tartarus. Sappho approaches.*

Sappho: I offered him my word, not my heart...
Seeking but to live a little longer,
And not into the afterlife depart
Before I've sated this erotic hunger,
I falsely swore my soul to serve
The Lord of Lies, which has perturbed
The sound and happy slumber of
My conscience. May love itself forgive
What I hath done, that it might live?
This burden is too great to bear!
For lust hangs heavy on the air,
I say, herein this dismal place:
One had best be aware of a grim,
Piscean race of growling devils.
They lure desirous souls t'wards
Ephemeral bait, and those who eat
Thereof their very lives forsake.

> *Sappho is momentarily entranced by an anglerfish's lure. She comes to her senses and pulls away just in time!*

O, I! Upon my wav'ring soul
Do stamp a firm decree:
Seek not illusionary lights
Whose flowers bear the seed
Of Hephaestus' dark Apocalypse.
Neither barren valleys wreathed
With gilded hate nor emerald greed
Which cloud and wayward lead
All souls who walk their paths.
Dark storms gnash and bleed;
Earth cracks and heaves; lights flicker,
Casting sinister reflections:
Blackest blackness flecked
With pallid, devil-tongued deceptions.
Yet harken to my death
Called Sirius, the Harvest Goddess!
In whose mournful eyes have I
Betrayed Diogenes, despite my promise—
Hephaestus has replaced the grisly truth
With pleasant lies; by my false conviction
Shall uphold his alibi!

Sirius: Of all creatures ... cometh Sappho ...
To seek my gracious blessing?
When Night has swallowed
Aught of worth to me?
I pray you'll stay a while; traverse
This dark, effulgent universe
Where anglerfish shall feed
Upon your god-forsaken dreams!
Your Pleasure has absconded
To some distant Northern province,

So I reprimand you, Sappho,
Fishing in this southern Tophet.
Here, devils shall ingratiate thee
With their yawning mouths;
Don't speak to them of mercy,
They shall drink your body down—
For you fled in the face of harm
And let my darling lover drown
Beneath the murmuring seas—
Thus I implore you to bequeath
Your soul to this infernal realm!
Too I, of vengeful temperament,
Will bid you this farewell:
The shaft of my swift bayonet,
That you might rot in Hell!

> *Sirius stabs Sappho in the side. She falls,
> injured, as the Anglerfish move in to engulf
> her.*

Sappho: Why have you betrayed me?
Sirius, I'll have you know
That even Death shan't stay me
From the Pleasure I adore!
Your gift shall be the end of me,
But pray, not for the time—
My task's not yet complete,
I must restore Voluptas' ailing mind …
And reveal the truth—the horrid truth!
For I did not abandon good Diogenes to Death:
Hephaestus stole me off with malicious intent!
Determined to be father of Apocalypse and Void,
'Twas he alone who slaughtered Hope and Joy.

Sirius arrests the Anglerfish with a gesture;
Hephaestus sheepishly slinks away...

Sirius: You lame and broken farrier
Who harrow all you touch!—
With hammer's crack and hiss,
Wrought wrongly by the wish
Of a malcontent, a murderer!
Though this Harvest Goddess
Harvests every human soul,
Sappho's, bold and modest,
Shall show miracles untold:
Arising from this deepest reach
Of aught that is malign, she shall
Grant to the Heav'ns a holy sign
Upon the beach, and rally the hearts
Of our unhappy humankind.
Meanwhile, I bid you to abide
Within the bowels of Hell
Till she has enjoined her bride,
Unhindered by your hateful tales!
Know empathy at last, and sin—
Of which you are the sole creator!—
Fly their world, and fast: the winds
Of karma turn upon thee, traitor!

Hephaestus flees the visage of his own conscience, pursued by growling devils. Sirius helps Sappho to her feet and speaks to her.

I pray you not to perish here;

Do not succumb to darkness!
But elevate thine corpse o'er
Yonder Hyperborean Mountains.
Sappho, flee this writhing hearse
And pour your pristine fountain
From the heights tomorrow morn:
For I am deaf to hallowed verse,
And blinded by the mortal curse
I drew out of my lover's failing form.
Yes, fly this dim-lit, deathly place
Which heaven has eschewed;
Fly we broken-hearted wraiths,
And pray for our renewal!
Fly, sweet Delphic queen!—
Towards the light!

ACT II, SCENE III

> *Sappho arrives upon the devastated beach,
> exhausted and clasping her wound. The
> corpses of Men lie scattered around her,
> remembering the gods' petty war.*

Sappho: I, risen out of Tartarus...
That dark, abysmal plane,
For naught but to discover
All the Earth's become a grave!
My poesy comes unravelled
At the seams: for death, as if
A hammer, hath dissolved
My soul's most-sound rock
To a morass of dust and gravel.

And yet my flesh, my mind!—
Has sworn upon Diana's pride
To journey to the distant North;
To end Hephaestus' reckless war
And become Voluptas' mortal bride.
That I shan't faint before arrival
At those far-flung snowy spires,
I seize within my soul a strength
To rival mighty Heracles—
And by it turn my back upon
These melancholy seas!
I'll northbound sojourn, sojourn,
Bravely, fiercely, free of fear,
And if felled by a swell of tears
Too deep to run from, shall divine
Their patterned waves and dream
With hopes to weave celestial rhyme.
For, Aurora Borealis shows her soul
To northern climes; diamond-dusts
The arctic air and beckon us to fly
With open arms about the tent-pole,
Once, twice 'round till dizzied Earth
Reveals the Light Divine....

> *As Sappho resolves to embark upon her impossible journey, the surviving Poets arrive carrying with them the sleeping Voluptas. Sappho bows in reverence before her.*

O queen of living eyes, I greet you;
Gleam beyond this glory-dawn!
I magnify my oath in season'd song:

Sappho reveals the songbook which Diana gave to her. As Sappho sings its scripture with the last of her strength, Voluptas awakes and is restored...

"O soul awake and
Sculpt an archéd shrine
Out 'yond the dross of pale
And fickle Time ...
Out past the loamy
Grip that brings to bear
A faded tombstone
Mouldered 'yond repair ...
Out past the scent of
Damp and rotted air,
Out 'yond the winter,
Spring is drawing near ...
For I have seen a
Sea of gilded stars,
Their aether crested
O'er this Earth of ours ...
And though the languid
Overcastted sky
Obscures them from
This Earth of yearning eyes ...
As I look upon your face,
Your perfect face, tonight,
All darkness turns to flesh ...
And blood ... and light."

Voluptas: These words are drawn of God,

And cause me softly to awaken ...
You sing to me a prophet's song,
A metered nectar taken
From the living cup of Zeus ...

Sappho: Drink, Voluptas, of this wine:
I yield my soul to you!
My spirit, like a min'ral spring,
A rushing aquifer, imbued
With love; which by your lips
Shall be eternally renewed.

> *Sappho falls into Voluptas' arms, exhausted on account of her wound.   Sappho faints; it appears that she is dead.*

ACT II, SCENE IV

> *The Poets have retired, leaving Voluptas alone with Sappho's body.   Diana Cervidae stands aside, and speaks in sombre tones...*

Diana: Oh sweet, naïve angel, whose
Whispered words and sighs
Have foiled the heavens' rouse
With faithful kindness; lies
Corrupted her for but a time,
But could not doom her soul
To an eternity of blindness.
For she so loved humanity—
At last, she had remembered!
Then stepped upon the shore

With feet so soft the cool sands
Speak their beauty to this day.
Beside the bleeding rivers
And the forests, fire-felled,
She knelt by her beloved seer
And shut her eyes for fear
She would espy her fallen friends.

Voluptas: I love you, dear.
Yet pray, ye Furies, hear me as
I speak your wretched names—
And defy you to bring suffering
Upon my favoured mortal bride!
She, my blue-eyed thaumaturge,
From whom the Muses learned
Their dearest secrets; I decree
Her and her fellows be released!
Flee! Into the hells with you!
I stake my rightful claim upon the seas,
Whose waters shall, in time, recede
And cease this stream of tears. For,
E'en the deepest sorrows shall abate!
The thoughts of Sappho shall
Be graven on an everlasting slate,
And history be elegantly forged;
All things which are not beautiful
Be purged through ardent labours,
Faithful strivings. Let all threads
Entangled be free and finely woven
Into perfectly delightful wholes!
So go your own way, gentle souls:
Seek the glorious taste of freedom!
Seek not wistful gods who would

Beseech you to believe in them;
But know me by my deeds, my friend—
I pray the Hells consume me in your stead;
I pray they strip my body of its sweetness
And temper my exuberance with meekness—
That you might wake;
That you might rise again.

Voluptas weeps and kisses Sappho. She stands and starts to wade into the sea, deeper and deeper, intent upon taking her life. Yet Sappho calls out, seemingly risen from death!

Sappho: Wait! I pray, do no such thing ...
For aught you wish, I wish the very same.

Voluptas: No, forsake all obsessions;
Scorn the vision of my face!
And know that I am written on your heart
And hereto shall be with you ... with you ...
Even in your very darkest hour.
And though that darkest hour,
Now drawing near,
May fill your mind with doubt;
Your heart with fear—
When the craft and the shipmen fail ...
Though all else fails, our love prevails.
For love, like the orient star,
Shall guide us safely home, where'er we are.

Sappho: Voluptas, I adore thee
And accept your gracious blessing;

Yet pray you to forgive me
Ling'ring doubtfulness distressing:
For, at every turn, I spy the summer;
Its light, which issues o'er the trees—
Yet wonder; yea I wonder,
In this tryst of Reverie and Reason,
Which shall hold dominion
O'er my funerary season?
For Reverie impels the soul
To dance—and dance with vigour!
Whilst Reason has insisted on
A higher degree of rigour!
Haunted by the shade of Disbelief,
I lack sufficient certainty;
And stricken by deficiency of faith,
Ponder o'er the likeness of eternity:
Is there aught that I might fear,
Or aught at all, which lies beyond
This deathly moment drawing near?
Has not the right I've done
Outstripped my many senseless wrongs,
That I should perish amorous and young?

Voluptas: Such fear of death Hephaestus bore
In fantasies and restless wars,
Gratuitous and sanguinary;
Let your Reason swiftly marry
Waning flesh to my immortal foil
That neither, e'er again, shall be despoiled.
For you, my mortal counterpart,
Were chosen not by merit but by birth
To dwell amongst the brightest stars.

Sappho: O bride, with whom I am enamoured,
Think me not a fool but be my guard
And course me quickly o'er the seas!
For fears now cause me quake,
And darkness clamours in my heart,
E'en though the Queen of Heaven
Spreads her vast, fair-golden wings
Over my eyes, and gives me dawning
Vision of the nearness of my spring....

> *Diana Cervidae reveals her true form to*
> *Sappho, by which she is stricken with wonder.*

Diana: By starlit skies, take bearings—
And make haste towards the light!
There your fathers and your sons
Unite, and lovers coalesce as One.
There you shall see beyond the seen
And know beyond the known:
Unbounded, bright and beautiful,
Of all misdeeds atoned.
For Love is in the eye of you,
And there the resurrection
Shall be writ in mystic ink
Upon your pupil's broad perfection.

Sappho: O, heaven's midst! My time
For Earth is passed and gives way
To a world unknown, unseen;
Like a crystal mountain stream
Made restless by a cresting wave
And cast into the sea! Thus,
All mortals, angels, gods

Cry, "Dei excelsior!"
For you, my love, this fleeting breath
Has sung an everlasting score;
The winds and the fires and the rains
Cry, "Glory... glory..."

> *Sappho takes Voluptas in her arms and sighs
> aloud, exhaling her terminal breath... Sappho
> dies.*

ACT II, SCENE V

> *The apocalypse is averted; the skies have
> cleared. Sappho's corpse rests upon the
> beach, beside Diogenes'.*

Diana: Smooth upon the stones she laid,
In ecstasy of yearning;
There once swelled ennobled
Breath within her, burning
For the hour of reunion.
Sacral glow upon her cheeks,
And knitted through her hair
The thread of heaven;
Gold leaf twined through locks so lustrous
Midnight pined for blackness such as hers.
Then swiftly, arm in arm with her,
Love snatched and soaréd yonder;
Bearings, by the sepulchre,
Set fast upon the fountain
Whence ambrosial nectars
Flow like seething rivers

273

Into the blameless oceans
Of our Lord; that final aureola,
Wherein armoured angels
In their legions dare not go,
Spread open, like a lover,
At the sight of Sappho's soul.
Yet evermore that prophet's song
Shall echo, 'spite her slumbers,
Clear to all who sleep upon
This Earth of light and wonder;
Through the night it follows them—
And further ... further still....

> *Diana takes Diogenes' corpse by the hand and slowly lifts him to his feet. Shocked and delighted, he examines his resurrected form.*

O soul, oft do you question
Where the end of life may lie?
Or hold ye bold pretension,
Founded on some prophet's clouded sight,
That unknown countries steal not upon you?

Diogenes: I ... I am alive!
Yet have cast off mortal flesh....

Diana: O soul, there is no life besides that
Which has passed the gate of Death;
Know too that Man is but a God
Corporeal, in earthen dress.
Now breathe! Ye gallant wings of fire;
O lovers' lungs effulgent scream!
Make for the spires of knowledge,

Pungent with a young girl's scent;
Drunk and love-struck, knived and kissed,
She draped the vast Pleroma o'er her mind
And scorned the mists of ignorance,
Even as they staked their claim
Upon her and her mortal soul.
Thus, if you'd know a single inch
Of heaven's metered whole,
May it be our Sappho's place of rest.

Diogenes: O, that in Diana's eyes
May I be seen a little worthy;
And humbly may she grant me
Merely this—merely this!
To join her in her Elysium tonight,
That I may greet my Sirius
And hold her hand in mine.
For pray, this corpse which
Lies before more penetrating eyes
Is naught but dust—the spirit flown
To distant worlds, to me unknown.

Diana: Then fly, marry your soul to them
And know their boundless wealth,
Yet know the True Desire of Man
Lies hidden still within himself!

> *Diogenes turns to see Sappho arise from the
> sleep of death, holding a shining star, beaming
> like the risen sun. He trembles before this
> beautiful vision.*

Diogenes: Tim'rous toned, the sun rose from
Behind the veiled horizon;
Morning on the shadowed plains
Stole soft and silently
O'er all men who'd dwelt
A season in their darkness.
Our enraptured gazes, shyly
Stricken by this Child of Aura,
Wept with trembling tears;
By grace, our risen prophet
Smiled upon the mended years.
Her back, Diana's caryatid,
Rendered Atlas obsolete
And soundly elevated o'er the seas
All life within their stirring waters
Through a single act of serendipity.
With cupped hands, bended,
All Men joined in heav'nly song;
Knelt upon the grasses tall,
With seed of emerald crown.
Drenched with dew of morning-tide,
They sang:

All Mortals: "Blesséd are the sorrowful!
Soon, theirs all honeyed harmonies shall be;
Theirs the gift ambrosial,
The gilded crown of Cupid's sting;
Theirs the choir inaudible,
Whose songs the papal masses sing.
And blesséd are the saddened hearts,
For them the kingdom cometh
On a wind with maiden countenance divine."

Voluptas: O smile,
Bring forth your trusting brightness:
All who love shall now be recombined!

> *Voluptas takes Sappho in her arms; they*
> *dance joyfully together. Diogenes and Sirius*
> *embrace, reunited at last!*

Chorus: O, Gods! With adoration do
We offer up our hearts to you,
Ye conquerors of gravity and sorrow;
Your sweet seraphic lyrics
Have been written on we multitudes
Who long to know the glory of the hour
Wherein our souls will dance
Upon your summer's sunlit glades;
When our shells will shatter
At the sight of you, and braided
Shafts of light will grace our endless days.
Naught shall stay this vision
From our eyes, nor cause to waver
'Midst the hardships and the hells
This joy which neither knavery
Nor lies are wont to falsely tell.
For Light has glowed effulgent
In the minds of all who've seen and heard,
The drama hidden in your heart;
A song of brightly coloured birds,
To which we sing with everlasting praise!

Diana: Sing supine and silently
To this and every starry night;
In them, scale and harmony

Shall fill you with divine delights
Which few have sought, and fewer still
Have known. Then pray we stars to guide
You safely back to hearth and home,
For there awaits the Earth, its joyful days,
Which Aurora wakens with her gentle rays.
Pray you now depart, and know their splendour,
T'wards which life must strive—and surrender!

ACT II, SCENE V

> *As the rapture of Elysium recedes into morning in the woods, the song of lovebirds echoes through the air; a doe dashes off into the distance; Diogenes' prostration transforms into a posture of sleep.... After a long while, he awakes, startled by the barking of a nearby bitch. He lights a lantern and holds it up high.*

Diogenes: Oh! Seems my Vestal goes a-roaming
Through the wood today—
A tragic tale came rolling
Off my tongue, before the spring!
Come ... it is morning, my queen!

Fin.

www.ingramcontent.com/pod-product-compliance
Lightning Source LLC
La Vergne TN
LVHW051040080426
835508LV00019B/1629